DIVREI MISHKAN HANEFESH
A Guide to the CCAR Machzor

דברי משכן הנפש

DIVREI MISHKAN HANEFESH

A Guide to the CCAR Machzor

Rabbi Edwin Goldberg, *Editor*

CENTRAL CONFERENCE OF AMERICAN RABBIS | 2016/5776

Library of Congress Cataloging-in-Publication Data

Names: Central Conference of American Rabbis, issuing body. | Goldberg, Edwin
C., editor.

Title: Divrei Mishkan haNefesh : a guide to the CCAR Machzor / Rabbi Edwin
Goldberg, editor.

Description: New York : CCAR Press, [2016] | © 2016 | Includes indexes.

Identifiers: LCCN 2016003481 (print) | LCCN 2016005304 (ebook) | ISBN
9780881232684 (pbk. : alk. paper) | ISBN 9780881232790 ()

Subjects: LCSH: Mahzor (Reform, Central Conference of American Rabbis). High
Holidays. | High Holidays--Liturgy. | Reform Judaism--Liturgy.

Classification: LCC BM675.H5 Z7195 2016 (print) | LCC BM675.H5 (ebook) | DDC
296.4/531--dc23

LC record available at http://lccn.loc.gov/2016003481

CCAR Press, 355 Lexington Avenue, New York, NY 10017
(212) 972-3636
www.ccarpress.org
Printed in U.S.A.
10 9 8 7 6 5 4 3 2 1

Acknowledgments

Like apples of gold in settings of silver is a word fitly spoken.
—Proverbs 25:11

D*ivrei Mishkan HaNefesh* has been a collaborative process from the start and I want to thank especially the other members of the original machzor editorial team: Rabbi Janet Marder, Rabbi Sheldon Marder, and Rabbi Leon Morris, as well as Cantor Evan Kent and Rabbi Elaine Zecher, and Rabbi Peter Berg. More than anyone else, the success of *Mishkan HaNefesh* is due to the tireless work and inexhaustible talent of Rabbi Hara Person, the publisher of the CCAR Press. I am so pleased that the team all answered my call to "get the band back together one more time" to produce this current volume.

I am also grateful to Rabbi Lawrence Hoffman, whose continued guidance informed so much of our work on the machzor and whose *Gates of Understanding II* (a commentary on *Gates of Repentance*) set such a high bar for books of this nature. In addition, Rabbi Richard Sarason has been a wonderful resource in matters of liturgy.

I would also like to thank those who diligently worked on the indexes— Rabbi Janet Marder, Leslie Rubin, and CCAR rabbinic intern Andrue Kahn—and Rabbi Lisa Edwards for her ideas about useful indexes. Thanks also to the CCAR Press team for all they do: Debbie Smilow, Ortal Bensky, Sasha Smith, Carly Linden, Rabbi Dan Medwin, and Rabbi Steven A. Fox, CCAR Chief Executive, as well as the same great production team that worked on *Mishkan HaNefesh*, Rabbi David E. S. Stein and Scott-Martin Kosofsky.

Finally, I want to thank Temple Sholom of Chicago for the opportunity to enhance my rabbinate with such a project as this book, and my loving family Melanie Cole Goldberg, Joseph Goldberg, and Benjamin Goldberg.

Contents

Part 3: Indexes and Tables

Introduction

> *T'shuvah is the chief goal of the Yamim Noraim, and a*
> *machzor is our indispensable manual and guide. We aim*
> *to create a machzor that will serve Reform Jews as they*
> *seek repentance, new direction, and a sense of return to*
> *God and the Jewish people.*
> —*from* A Vision Statement for a New Reform Machzor

I. Twenty-first century life in America offers many blessings, especially in the field of technology. Nevertheless, the ability to do more without a value-laden context is frightening. Some fear we are turning ourselves into something akin to the Sorcerer's Apprentice. Edna St. Vincent Millay was prophetic when she wrote (in 1939):

> Upon this gifted age, in its dark hour,
> Rains from the sky a meteoric shower
> Of facts . . . they lie unquestioned, uncombined.
> Wisdom enough to leech us of our ill
> Is daily spun, but there exists no loom
> To weave it into fabric . . .

In short, we post-moderns need a corrective, "a reset" that centers us in a context of what matters most. Life, many of us deem, is a problem. Jewish text and tradition—presented as a meaningful, relevant High Holy Day experience—can be a captivating and vital solution.

Mishkan HaNefesh, the new prayer book, was designed as a sacred tool for exciting and transformative worship on Rosh HaShanah and Yom Kippur. The book seeks to meet people where they are, presenting diverse views of God with a respectful yet fresh approach to tradition, framed in the following ways:

- An unwavering commitment to the equality of men and women;
- Attention paid to the present-day concerns, fears, and hopes of the people who will pray from these pages;

- Fidelity to the ethical dimension of Judaism; embracing of the universal and the particular;
- An effort to deal with the tension between the historical theology of the High Holy Days (God's sovereignty and judgment) and more contemporary beliefs, such as the "theology of human adequacy."

The High Holy Days are *complex* by their very nature. Nevertheless, this book was designed to be used as a sacred implement in public worship without being too *complicated*. There are many choices to be made in employing the machzor, but the unifying principle is simple: what matters is not "mastering" the book, but rather allowing the book to help us experience transformative, sacred moments.

The name of the new machzor is significant: *Mishkan* (sacred dwelling-place) at the same time evokes the holy practice of Jewish people and their families engaged in communal worship in a particular space, and it also emphasizes the continuity with the Reform Shabbat and weekday prayer book *Mishkan T'filah*. The second word, *HaNefesh* (the soul), reflects a specific truth: the most fundamental "work" of these Days of Awe must be performed by the individual. Indeed, although many traditional sources see the ultimate goal of these days as convincing God to treat us with compassion even when we fail, the focus of our prayer book is on the equally compelling message of our own *cheshbon hanefesh*, the accounting of our soul. Especially in this modern era, the privileging of our own responsibility to change over our hope in God's compassion seems appropriate. This focus on the individual encourages the worshiper to enjoy time engrossed in prayer or reflection, even if the congregation as a whole has moved on to a new page. Personal experience, in consort with public worship, is a guiding principle of the machzor.

II. What is the guiding principle of *Divrei Mishkan HaNefesh*, this volume about *Mishkan HaNefesh*? Think of it as a sort of midrash on the machzor, a "*Mishkan HaNefesh* Rabbah." Like a midrashic compilation, the aim of this volume is to provide both exegetical and homiletical material: *chomer l'hasbir v'chomer lidrosh*. Also similar to midrashic collections, the framing structure will be somewhat idiosyncratic. The

purpose of the work is not to be encyclopedic or exhaustive but rather to
serve as a springboard for entering into the sanctuary of our souls with
enthusiasm and helpful insights, tips, and guideposts.

This book focuses on the prayers and scriptural offerings included
in *Mishkan HaNefesh*. Rubric by rubric, insights are presented with
background information concerning the perspective and choices of the
editors, as well as an offering of extra material to engage the reader (as
well as provide *chomer* for the worship leader).

A number of brief essays are included, composed by the members
of the machzor core editorial team. They expand on certain editorial
choices and approaches. There are a number of useful indexes and
tables as well, including of the poetry selections, biblical and Rabbinic
citations, and commentaries.

Rest assured that, at the core of this book, you will find answers to
basic questions asked on behalf of those charged with creating meaningful worship experiences with the aid of *Mishkan HaNefesh*. These
include such questions as:

- Why were certain changes made?
- What should I do about these changes?
- What philosophical or theological approach underlies
  these changes?

In addition, the conversation about the greater challenge of the Days of
Awe is reflected in references to other texts and interpretations.

What this volume does *not* do is repeat the material presented in
Mishkan HaNefesh. There is also a plethora of material already available
in the books *Machzor: Challenge and Change* (two volumes) as well as
Ravblog, and of course the many other classic and modern commentaries
on the liturgy of the Days of Awe.

To paraphrase Rashi's famous philosophy: this volume focuses on the
elements of the new machzor that say, *"Darsheini!"* Hopefully, a few
words, fitly spoken, will help in your preparation for these sacred,
vital days.

Mishkan HaNefesh:
Ten Things That You Need To Know

The creation of a new prayer book for the Days of Awe presents a challenge as well as an opportunity. The opportunity is great worship and transformed worshipers. The challenge is how to use the book in all its complexity without it being too complicated. To help the first-time user, here are some important things to know:

1   The book continues *Mishkan T'filah*'s "integrated theology" approach. This means that the majority of the book features the "two-page" spread, wherein the right side reflects a more traditional rendering and the left side a more creative theological approach. Some sections of the service (or in the case of *Yizkor*, the entire service) are linear and have no two-page spreads.

2   The right-side translations are "faithful" but not literal, recognizing there is no way to render a word literally from Hebrew into English. The best one can do is a translation that reflects the Hebrew and the nuance of English. For more on our approach to translation, see "Translating Faith" on page 85.

3   The machzor was not created to be used "as is." In other words, like *Mishkan T'filah*, the worship leader(s) should prepare a particular set of choices concerning the two-page spread, as well as other features described below. It should also be understood that no prayer book can ever be more than a sacred implement in the facilitation of a worship experience, even as no textbook guarantees a wonderful lesson.

4   In addition to the left-side readings, which are marked by a gray background (or "wash"), there are pages with a blue background, set off with a black border. These in general are meant to be read silently.

5   To some extent, *Mishkan HaNefesh* retains the practice assumed in *Mishkan T'filah* that reaching the Hebrew blessing

at the bottom of a page serves as a sign to turn to the next page, hence allowing for fewer page announcements from the bimah. However, unlike *Mishkan T'filah*, many more pages are linear.

6 *Mishkan HaNefesh* offers suggested alternative Torah readings for Rosh HaShanah and Yom Kippur, explained in a separate essay.

7 The Yom Kippur daytime services need not be prayed in the order found in the machzor; indeed, many congregations may choose to employ only certain elements in any given year. They may choose as well to supplement a service with a teaching or panel discussion.

8 Significant *Mishkan HaNefesh* innovations include:
   • The shofar service for Rosh HaShanah morning is divided into three sections, each one in a different part of the service. This helps the worshiper focus more time and energy on each theme of the shofar service.
   • Suggested alternative Torah readings.
   • The Yom Kippur volume contains a newly conceived *Avodah* service, based on fifteen steps of ascent and holiness.
   • The Yom Kippur volume offers a *Minchah* service with a special theme of Jewish ethical/spiritual values (*midot*).
   • The *Yizkor* service reflects a theme of seven lights of mourning and remembrance.
   • The *Eileh Ezk'rah* service offers a completely new and innovative approach by remembering those men and women whose lives and deaths were examples of moral choices made in service of repairing the world: *tikkun olam*.
   • The *N'ilah* service reflects a general theme of God's outstretched hand.

9 Individual worshipers are encouraged to explore the book on their own and at their own pace—even if that means they do not keep up with the congregation because they have been drawn to a particular commentary or reading.

10 Responsive readings are not indicated with italics. Instead, the worship leader is invited to suggest certain readings to be read responsively, if so wished.

Profiles of the Editors of *Mishkan HaNefesh*

RABBI EDWIN GOLDBERG

Rabbi Edwin Goldberg serves as the senior rabbi of Temple Sholom of Chicago. He received rabbinic ordination and a doctorate in Hebrew Literature from the Hebrew Union College–Jewish Institute of Religion (in 1989 and 1994, respectively). He is the author of many books, including: *Midrash for Beginners*; *Heads and Tales: Stories of the Sages to Enlighten Our Minds*; *Swords and Plowshares: Jewish Views of War and Peace*; *Love Tales from the Talmud*, and *Saying No and Letting Go: Jewish Wisdom on Making Room for What Matters Most*.

Rabbi Goldberg served as the coordinating editor of *Mishkan HaNefesh*. He is married to Melanie Cole Goldberg, a Jewish educator.

▶ Rabbi Goldberg wanted to work on the new machzor because he felt that the High Holy Days—when done well—provide a powerful experience for lay people and clergy alike. It was time for a new sacred tool, a machzor that reflected the style of *Mishkan T'filah* and offered a wide choice of theological perspectives that suited the more formal atmosphere of the Days of Awe.

RABBI JANET MARDER

Since 1999, Rabbi Janet Marder has served as Senior Rabbi of Congregation Beth Am of Los Altos, California. During her years there, she has focused on worship renewal, expanding the circle of Torah learning, and involving members in the work of pastoral care. She loves to help learners apply Jewish insights to the challenges of adult life, such as marriage, dealing with adult children, finding meaning, and facing mortality.

Following ordination in 1979, she pursued graduate studies in the Department of Comparative Literature at UCLA, specializing in Modern Hebrew and Yiddish Literature. In April 2003 she was elected the first woman president of the Central Conference of American Rabbis. She is a Senior Rabbinic Fellow of the Shalom Hartman Institute in Jerusalem.

► Rabbi Marder accepted the invitation to be an editor of *Mishkan HaNefesh* because she loves language, literature, and experiencing prayer. She was also looking forward to spending more time with her husband, Rabbi Sheldon Marder.

RABBI SHELDON MARDER

Ordained in 1978 (Hebrew Union College–Jewish Institute of Religion), Rabbi Sheldon Marder has served the Jewish Home of San Francisco since 1999. In that setting he teaches Torah, art, and poetry, while providing Jewish spiritual care for older adults with serious illness. His published essays on spiritual care include: "God Is in the Text: Using Sacred Text and Teaching in Jewish Pastoral Care"; "Psalms, Songs & Stories: Music and Midrash at the Jewish Home of San Francisco"; and "Doorways of Hope: Adapting to Alzheimer's." He is a coeditor, translator, and writer of *Mishkan HaNefesh*, and a Senior Rabbinic Fellow of the Shalom Hartman Institute in Jerusalem.

► Rabbi Marder's interest in working on *Mishkan HaNefesh* stemmed from a lifelong love of Jewish prayer books, poetry, and the Reform Movement.

RABBI LEON MORRIS

Rabbi Leon A. Morris is a vice president for Israel programs at the Shalom Hartman Institute of North America. A leading educator in the field of adult Jewish study, Rabbi Morris made *aliyah* to Israel with his family in June 2014, after serving as the rabbi of Temple Adas Israel in Sag Harbor, New York. He was the founding director of the Skirball Center for Adult Jewish Learning at Temple Emanu-El in Manhattan. He served as an editor on *Mishkan HaNefesh*.

► Rabbi Morris's desire to be involved in creating the new machzor for the Reform Movement grew out of his own experience as a rabbi. He had the privilege of working in two different professional roles: serving as a founding executive director for an adult educational institution in Manhattan that attempts to cultivate liberal Jews for whom *talmud torah* is a core component of their Jewish identity; and as a congregational rabbi for a small but growing Reform synagogue in the Hamptons. These two professional homes have resulted in a dynamic tension that he felt would serve this project well—an intense love for classic Jewish texts balanced by a deep understanding of Reform Jews and current modes of Reform worship.

For the team's work together, Rabbi Morris was primarily interested in applying a "hermeneutic of embrace" as we looked to the classic machzor as our starting point—to give new meaning to ancient words, to creatively revive the poetry of the Jewish people, and, through commentary and study texts, connect contemporary Jews to the inherited texts of our liturgy. As the team began their work, he felt strongly that a theological litmus test for everything that appears in the prayer book is passé. A new Reform machzor would need to encourage congregants to engage with its words on multiple levels, empowering every Reform worshiper to participate in the process of interpretation. He wanted to help create a machzor that would not shy away from dialectic and paradox, that would reflect a real love for unique components of the inherited liturgy of the High Holy Days.

CANTOR EVAN KENT

A graduate of the Manhattan School of Music and HUC-JIR DFSSM (1988), Cantor Evan Kent made *aliyah* to Israel in 2013. He lives in Jerusalem with his husband, Rabbi Donald Goor, and their cat Merlin. He is currently on the faculty of HUC-JIR Jerusalem and also teachers at the Levinsky School of Education in Tel Aviv.

Cantor Kent served as cantor at Temple Isaiah, Los Angeles, for twenty-five years; and he also served on the faculty of HUC-JIR LA for fifteen years. He recently received his doctorate in music education from Boston University. His doctoral research examined how music at Jewish summer camps in North America aids in the development of Jewish identity.

► Cantor Kent writes in retrospect: "One of my personal axioms for religious and liturgical life is the words of Rav Kook: 'May the old become new, and the new become holy.' As I became aware that an editorial team for the machzor was in formation, I realized that a cantorial voice and perspective needed to be on the committee. My position as a member of the editorial committee has been twofold: to ensure that tradition has been fairly portrayed within the pages of the machzor, and that the machzor affords the prayer leaders and congregants opportunities for musical and liturgical creativity."

RABBI ELAINE ZECHER

Rabbi Elaine Zecher has served Temple Israel of Boston since 1990. She also served as the Chair of the CCAR Worship and Practices Committee for over a decade. She worked on *Mishkan T'filah* and chaired the Machzor Advisory Group for *Mishkan HaNefesh*. She also was part of the Editorial Team Advisors for the machzor. She is Vice President for Leadership of the CCAR Board. Rabbi Zecher's rabbinate has focused on teaching and mining Judaism's rich resources to nurture the inner life of the individual, as well as of the community.

► Rabbi Zecher writes in retrospect: "It has been an honor to work on *Mishkan HaNefesh*. Professor Henry Slonimsky wrote that the Jewish soul is mirrored in the prayer book. I think this is also true with the machzor. To be able to contribute to the individual and the community's soul-searching experience during the High Holy Days is a great privilege. I have learned a great deal and deepened my own faith and connection to Judaism through the process of developing the machzor. Working with this particular editorial team has brought me great joy and insight into liturgy, prayer, and the spiritual life of the Jewish people."

RABBI HARA PERSON

Rabbi Hara Person is the Publisher of CCAR Press, and the CCAR Director of Strategic Communications. She works with CCAR leadership and members to produce books and other publications for rabbis, congregations, and the Jewish community. She served as Executive Editor of

Mishkan HaNefesh. Her essays and poems have been published in various anthologies, journals, and on-line platforms.

▶ Rabbi Person writes in retrospect: "It was an unbelievable experience to work on *Mishkan HaNefesh,* from envisioning it as an abstract concept to holding the printed book in my hands. And it was truly an inspiration to work with and learn from this incredible group of colleagues who made up the editorial team, as well as to learn from all the colleagues and congregants who contributed ideas and feedback throughout the process."

Part 1
Commentary

Rosh HaShanah Evening Service

Avinu Malkeinu, renew us.

As explained in the Introduction to *Mishkan HaNefesh*, each service in the machzor begins with a thematic phrase that seeks to highlight the essence of the service. The goal is not to reduce a service to one line but to help the worshiper grasp a major motif. "Avinu Malkeinu, renew us" serves as the phrase for Rosh HaShanah evening. These words encapsulate the essential message of the Days of Awe. We are gathered to ask that God's judgmental side (*Malkeinu*) be diminished just as God's compassionate side (*Avinu*) be heightened. Ideally, we would mirror this transformation in our own attitudes toward others and ourselves.

Opening the Book
Don't be surprised if some High Holy Day worshipers, being used to *Gates of Repentance*, are bewildered by the book's opening the "wrong" way. Depending on the culture of your community, this might require some education.

About Italics
Italics in *Mishkan HaNefesh* indicate scriptural verses and not responsive reading. Responsive reading is always an option in the book. It is up to the service leader to invite the congregation to participate in such a way. *A leader may have to explain to the congregation that italics don't equal responsive reading.* Nor does non-italics indicate text that only one person can read. Some readings have indented paragraphs to make responsive reading easier to facilitate.

Pages 2–5: For Study and Reflection

We could fill volumes of books with texts meant for study and reflection and still not scratch the surface of inspirational material. These few blue-shaded pages (suggesting a practice of silent study rather than communal reading) are simply a taste of *chomer* for meditation. You will note that, as in *Mishkan T'filah*, there are rubric labels, or sidebars, on the margins, to help the worshiper follow the structure of the service.

Pages 6–9: Songs and Poems

The options here are designed for group participation. The second offering, *Hashiveinu*/Return Again, which may be sung to the melody by

Rabbi Shlomo Carlebach, often "returns" in the service. Congregations may choose to use it like a reprise in a musical, tracking the service back to this major message of the Days of Awe. Both modern and ancient songs are also included in the following pages. (On opening songs, see also the discussion by Cantor Evan Kent, below, p. 119.)

Pages 10–11: Candlelighting

True to the philosophy of *Mishkan HaNefesh*, we offer choices for the candlelighting reading. All follow the principle that "the numinous is luminous," that is, we can find spiritual meaning in the metaphor of light.

Pages 12–13: Opening Prayers

Two pieces are offered here. The prayer on page 12 uses the title of a painting (at the Art Institute of Chicago). "This Autumn Night" (page 13) was inspired by a prayer of the early American Reform rabbi David Einhorn. This reading reflects the desire of the editors to include legacy pieces from our Reform Jewish past.

Page 15: Sounding of the Shofar

Why sound the shofar on Rosh HaShanah evening? Well, for one thing, many congregations already do. Moreover, there is something appealing about the notion of the shofar's blast heralding the declaration of the New Year. So why wait? However, this is only a suggestion—and congregations may choose to wait until the next day to sound the shofar.

Pages 16–19: *Hin'ni*

Long removed from the Musaf service that is no longer included in Reform liturgical practice, we followed the tradition of *Gates of Repentance* by featuring *Hin'ni* here. Both the leaders of the worship service (usually the cantor) and the individual participants (i.e., the *nefesh* in *Mishkan HaNefesh*) are invited to consider their inadequacies in light of God's expectations for us. In the past, prayer leaders prayed vicariously for the congregation as well as for themselves. The Hebrew for the prayer leader (p. 17) features gender choices, and this may affect the musical accompaniment. In offering this personal *Hin'ni*, *Mishkan HaNefesh* offers the opportunity for personal reflection at this moment as a parallel to the worship leader's prayer before the ark. The innovation of the personal

Hin'ni is a corrective and counterweight to the tradition of the prayer leader "taking center stage" since the *Hin'ni* has been experienced by many as a solo performance.

SH'MA AND ITS BLESSINGS

You will note that the running head at the top of the page and the sidebars running down the right and left margins change here, signifying a new section of the service.

Pages 20–21: *Bar'chu*

Following the pattern of integrated theology first featured in *Mishkan T'filah*, this two-page spread offers the traditional call of worship on the right side and more theologically expansive, alternative choices on the left. (For more on integrated theology, see the essay by Rabbi Elaine Zecher on p. 113.) For instance, there is the association of God with the kabbalistic name "the Infinite." The notes below the line are designed to inform, but not overly distract the worshiper from the prayer itself.

Pages 26–31: *Sh'ma*

You will notice that the *Baruch Shem* line is set in a smaller font and in a different color. This acknowledges the custom of saying the second line in a whisper. (Yom Kippur is the exception; there, the font is the same size as the *Sh'ma*.)

The first sentence on the top of page 26 is one of many times that the central lesson of the Days of Awe is referenced: *the God of judgment (Elohim) is also the God of mercy (Adonai)*. Beginning with the *Sh'ma* and continuing with *Avinu Malkeinu*, the Thirteen Midot, and finally the seven repetitions of *Adonai Hu HaElohim* intoned at the conclusion of Yom Kippur, this essential theme appears as the leitmotif that runs throughout the machzor and the Days of Awe themselves.

In the Rosh HaShanah Evening Service, the Hebrew text of the second paragraph of the *Sh'ma* is not included. Nevertheless, the English translation of these words is presented on the left side (p. 29). Throughout the machzor, as well as in the earlier *Mishkan T'filah*, there is a tension between presenting the traditional text while not alienating worshipers with the cruel reality of a theology punctuated by reward and punishment. This is one of many cases where, in effect, we suggest that words be taken seriously though not necessarily literally.

This is the first of many instances in the machzor in which we make important statements about the centrality of environmental/ecological concerns in the 21st century. The centrality of this theme is intentional. The sublinear comment on page 29 makes the point—and other prayers in both volumes continue the theme.

Pages 32–33: *Emet ve-Emunah*

This is another good example of integrated theology and the two-page spread. God saves us from tyranny (p. 32), but we also possess the means to free ourselves from figurative "Egypts" (p. 33).

Pages 34–35: *Mi Chamocha*

The reading on page 35 by Viktor Frankl invites the worshiper to consider liberation from many different historic and existential perspectives.

Pages 36–37: *Hashkiveinu*

Please note that, unlike in *Mishkan T'filah*, the description of God as Ruler (*Malkeinu*), which might be read as King, has been retained from the traditional liturgy. This choice was not meant as a step back from a gender-inclusive understanding of God (*Shomreinu*), but simply a recognition that on the Days of Awe, and especially Rosh HaShanah, the imagery of God as the Ultimate Ruler is both prevalent and relevant in the text.

Professional decorum prevented the name of the author of the beautiful poem on page 37 from being listed, but I am calling on editorial privilege here: it is Rabbi Hara Person. And it is a masterpiece.

Pages 38–39: Shabbat Inserts

Page 39 features two pieces on stopping to enjoy nature. Neither were written by Jews. During the piloting, some voiced concerns about whether non-Jewish authors have a place in a Jewish prayer book. The editors disagreed. As the ancient adage puts it, Torah was given to Jews but wisdom was given to all. We can find great spiritual wisdom in the writings of many non-Jewish thinkers. Unless they possessed some affront to Jewish sensibilities, we chose to include pieces like these—and were proud of that decision.

Page 40: *Chatzi Kaddish*

Worshipers who are used to *Gates of Repentance* and are using this book for the first time may very well stumble over the addition to the Kaddish: *ul·eila mikol* (entirely), in reference to God's transcendent nature. We felt that retrieving this phrase, part of the common parlance in non-Reform settings, was an important way to recognize the present "High" part of the High Holy Days. The sublinear note places the restoration in perspective.

Page 41: Personal Prayer

The author of this prayer, Rabbi Norman Hirsh, provides insight into the line "Except that Love makes itself small." He writes: "It is in the nature of divine and human love to make itself small."

HAT'FILAH

Pages 42–43: *Kavanah*

Page 43 features a new reading that was created by adapting various traditional sources, which are cited in the sublinear notes. Rabbi Sheldon Marder and Rabbi Janet Marder were responsible for most of these pieces—and their mastery of nuance, as well as tradition, is a prime factor in this book's efficacy.

Pages 46–47: *G'vurot*

In the Hebrew, *Mishkan HaNefesh* continues the practice from *Mishkan T'filah* of allowing the worshiper to choose between the traditional wording, *m'chayeih hameitim*, and the Reform version, *m'chayeih hakol*. *Mishkan T'filah* placed the traditional *hameitim* in parentheses. For this volume we chose to use a slash mark ("/") in order to give equal weight to either option. It is also worth noting that we offer an English version that

Transliteration Note
In the transliteration, the editors have chosen to render the *tzeirei* vowel with the long sound ("*ei*") and not the shorter pronunciation practiced by Israelis ("*e*"). Our feeling was that a North American book should reflect North American practice.

enables everyone to pray together, without making a theological choice, by speaking about "all life" as well as "from life to death." Perhaps this is a truly "integrated theology" because it integrates disparate ideas and recognizes that all of our words about God are equally metaphoric, equally inadequate, and equally valuable.

Pages 48–52: *K'dushat HaShem*
A feature unique to the Days of Awe liturgy is the three *Uvchein* declarations. Our version restores the mention of David, not because we ascribe to the messianic teachings of Rabbinic Judaism but because we want a vision of the messianic age to be present in this book.

Pages 56–57: *K'dushat HaYom*
The tension between a distant, removed Monarch and an immanent Presence cannot be resolved by our High Holy Day worship experience; it can only be acknowledged. The declaration *m'loch* in large font places this tension in the center of our thoughts. The classical liturgy of page 56 is countered on page 57 by a more human-centered interpretation of this tension.

Page 70: *Oseh Shalom*
All of the *Oseh Shalom* prayers in *Mishkan HaNefesh* feature the added phrase *kol yoshvei teiveil*, from Isaiah 18:3 and Psalm 33:8. (*Mishkan T'filah* likewise features this addition after *HaT'filah*, although not as part of the *Kaddish Yatom*.) Our purpose in this not-insignificant change was to reflect the Reform Movement's dedication *l'takein olam b'malchut Shaddai*, to work for a world of peace and justice, not just for the Jewish community. We reflected this value with these additional words. Such an addition has become common in newer liberal liturgies. It is possible that Rabbi Zalman Schachter-Shalomi and his Jewish Renewal Movement are responsible for introducing the phrase. On universalism in *Mishkan HaNefesh*, see Rabbi Lawrence Hoffman's essay on the subject, pages xxviii–xxix in the machzor.

Pages 72–73: *Mi Shebeirach*
In a change from *Mishkan T'filah*, this new machzor features a number

of different prayers for healing. Page 73 offers a beautiful example from Cantor Leon Sher. For those who wish to sing the Debbie Friedman version, it can be found in the Morning Service, on page 245.

Pages 74–77: *Avinu Malkeinu*

In homage to Rabbi Jeff Salkin, who was actually speaking of Saturday morning soccer when he coined the original phrase, I have adapted his teaching as follows: "The God of Max Janowski is a zealous God." By this I mean that his version of *Avinu Malkeinu*, made even more famous by Barbra Streisand, is here to stay. Therefore, every time *Avinu Malkeinu* appears in the machzor, the words used by Janowski are presented together. Sometimes they are at the end of *Avinu Malkeinu* (as we see on page 77) and sometimes not.

As is commonly known, a reference to *Avinu Malkeinu* first appears in the Talmud (*Taanit* 25b), purporting to go back to well-known authorities in the second century CE. From the beginning, it was understood to be an appeal for God's mercy:

> Rabbi Eliezer once stood before the ark [during a drought] and recited the twenty-four benedictions for fast days but his prayer was not answered. Rabbi Akiva stood there after him and proclaimed: "Avinu Malkeinu, our Father, our King, we have no King but You; our Father, our King, have mercy upon us"—and rain fell. . . .

We have also added traditional verses to *Avinu Malkeinu* not found in *Gates of Repentance*. In other services you will see various translations of *Avinu Malkeinu*. Our editorial committee was committed to maintaining the centrality of *Avinu Malkeinu* in our machzor, while also presenting alternative theological choices within it—a recurrent concern that we applied to other prayers, as well.

We also wanted to make sure that worshipers do not see the many repetitions of *Avinu Malkeinu* as redundant. To be sure, some Jews view its regularized recitation positively: a familiar signpost throughout the long set of services or a trance-inducing experience (in a good way). Nevertheless, the sensibility of many of our congregants dictated a more nuanced, selective approach.

In keeping with this sort of calculus, our committee varied the

Interconnected Questions

Issues regarding *Avinu Malkeinu* revolved around a set of interconnected questions.

- Are some verses no longer necessary, or even objection-able?
- Do some speak to our human condition more than others?
- And, can we afford to offer a text that does not sync with the widely used and justifiably beloved version composed by Max Janowski (and famously sung by Barbra Streisand)?

Avinu ("our Father") represents God's compassion. *Malkeinu* ("our King") signifies God's stern, judgmental face. Taken together, *Avinu Malkeinu* asks that God's judgment be tempered by God's mercy.

The theme of moving God from judgment to mercy is widespread throughout the Days of Awe; but it is also, by extension, a theme applied to us, as well as to God. Just as we seek God's compassion, so should we show compassion to one another—and to ourselves. Of course, many of us find objectionable the core idea that a drought is brought on by God as punishment for moral failings; and then there's the notion that punishment persists until we successfully petition God to bring it to an end.

Our editorial committee wanted to make sure that worshipers not see the many repetitions of *Avinu Malkeinu* as redundant. To be sure, some Jews find its regularized recitation positive: a familiar signpost throughout the long set of services or a trance-inducing experience (in the best sense). Nevertheless, the sensibility of many worshipers dictated a more nuanced, selective approach.

rendition of *Avinu Malkeinu* to fit the mood of the particular services in which it is featured. At the outset of the Days of Awe, the declarations here avoid too specific a focus on the manifold ways we have missed the mark. Subsequent occurrences of the prayer seek to engage the worshiper in a deeper repentant mood.

Earlier piloting featured our attempt to not use the word "sin" in the translation of *Avinu Malkeinu*. A number of colleagues felt the word "sin" was tainted by the Moral Majority as a condemnation of homosexuality. In addition, the word has Christian connotations. Avoiding the word "sin" in the machzor is not easy, since the Hebrew word *cheit* is universally recognized as "sin." We thought about substituting "missed the mark" for "sin"—a technically correct translation, as the Hebrew comes from the imagery of archery and the errant arrow. However, we concluded that this choice would not do justice to the overall sentiment of the Days of Awe. This was reinforced by the feedback received from several rounds of piloting. We also tried out a different approach, translating the word as "brokenness." In the end we kept the word "sin," despite many people's discomfort with an English word that sounds problematic to some ears. But we did not simply retain "sin." The verse carefully says: "*Avinu Malkeinu*, we have strayed and sinned before You." The word "strayed" is important here: it is an attempt to capture the sense of the Hebrew word *cheit*—as sin, but also as "missing the mark" or "departing from the straight path."

We did decide to render the final declaration of *Avinu Malkeinu* as "our deeds are wanting" and not "we have no merit." Self-abasement can easily be seen as its own form of spiritual narcissism. The purpose of this language is to avoid that.

It is also important to point out that we use a non-gendered translation of *Avinu Malkeinu*. The phrase "Almighty and Merciful" was suggested to us by the poet and translator Chana Bloch as a non-gendered way to convey the sense of "Father" and "King." This phrase has the poetic beauty of replicating the sound and rhythm of the Hebrew, in the number of syllables and in the opening sound of each word. "Almighty and Merciful" also evokes the same qualities as King (almighty) and Father (merciful).

CONCLUDING PRAYERS

Pages 82–85: *Aleinu*

We have restored the traditional text to the logical position of the top of page 82. In *Mishkan T'filah*, this most popular, and traditional, rendition was not the first piece on the upper right side of the page spread, leading to a great deal of confusion among worshipers. Two more universal renderings are presented as alternative options on page 83.

Pages 86–91: Kaddish

The pre-*Kaddish* readings range from old classics to new favorites. In general we sought a balance between "legacy" pieces and more contemporary renderings. (Legacy pieces are prayers that are beloved especially by older congregants, or those that reflect the writings of great Reform Jews of the past.)

The sublinear note on page 89 is a favorite of mine, although a scholar of Rabbi Eliyahu HaKohen may object that we are placing the line out of context. But we have sought to privilege spiritual effect over academic or historical accuracy. What *Legends of the Jews* actually says (vol. 1, p. 43) is:

> The grasshopper also has a lesson to teach to man. All the summer through it sings, until its belly bursts, and death claims it. Though it knows the fate that awaits it, yet it sings on. So man should do his duty toward God, no matter what the consequences.

As Rabbi Richard Sarason has noted, the traditional lesson from the grasshopper drawn in the source is not the modern lesson that we should sing in the face of death. Rather, it is that we should do our duty to God.

The source of the tradition (noted in *Legends*, vol. 5, n. 192) is *Sheivet Musar*, 22, 70b and 73c, as well as 31, 98a. *Sheivet Musar* is an eighteenth-century Ottoman work by Rabbi Elijah b. Solomon Abraham HaKohen of Smyrna, first published in Ladino in 1748.

Pages 90–91: *Kaddish Yatom*

On the two additions to this prayer (*ul·eila mikol* and *kol yoshvei teiveil*), see notes to pages 40 and 70, above.

Pages 92–97: Closing Songs

We included not only the old favorites but also an excerpt from Psalm 27, reflecting its timeliness throughout the month of Elul and during the Days of Awe, as well as *Hashiveinu*/Return Again. (On closing songs, see also the discussion by Cantor Evan Kent, below, p. 119.)

Pages 98–99: Blessings for the New Year

We included an acrostic blessing and an intimation of things to come: a reference to the seal as well as the inscription in the Book of Life.

Doing It Right or Doing It Well, *Which?*

At one point in the Harry Potter series, Dumbledore lets Harry know that there will come a time when he has to choose between what is right and what looks easy. The point he is making is that Voldemort chose the easy over the right; of course Harry should do the opposite. The right choice is clearly the moral one.

When it comes to the creation of *Mishkan HaNefesh*, the editors were instructed by Rabbi Lawrence Hoffman to consider a different choice, but one that has its detractors on either side. In short, when it comes to relevant liturgy we had to choose between doing it right or doing it well. As explained in his piece in the summer 2013 *CCAR Journal*, "Doing it Right or Doing it Well?" rightness is about following the rules. Doing it well is responding to the experience of the worshiper. Of course, the departures from the rules did not need to be radical. We didn't need to declare *Eit laasot l'Adonai* and for the sake of God overturn everything, but we had to display common sense.

I thought of this as I remembered looking at the traditional Yom Kippur liturgy and omitting countless repetitions of the Thirteen *Midot*. The Thirteen *Midot* are about as fundamental a text to the Days of Awe as anything. But they do not have to be repeated more than five or six times in a given day.

What are some more subtle examples of how the editors omitted sometimes important prayers in order to privilege more important pieces? Understanding that there is a limit to how much any given volume can contain, as well as our commitment to an integrated theology along with two-page spreads, the choices were not always easy, but they were necessary. So for instance, the Torah services in *Mishkan HaNefesh* omit some verses, such as *Ki Mitziyon*. We had nothing against this declaration; we just needed to cut somewhere. The same was true of *Gates of Repentance*. They cut out Genesis 21 from the Rosh HaShanah Torah reading. We were not prepared to lose that again.

We also didn't include the full traditional verses of the *Sh'ma* every time. Many beautiful *piyutim* were not included. The Torah and haftarah portions feature very limited commentary.

Not including things was not easy. (We took comfort in knowing that many congregations will avail themselves of screen technology—if not today, then in the future—and omissions can be corrected on the screens, or with the old standby, handouts.) It was not ideal, but then we could only produce a sacred tool to help present effective and meaningful worship. There will never be a "just add water" prayer book.

An old sermon title has a great name: "Steering or Drifting, Which?" The editors of *Mishkan HaNefesh* wrestled with a different but potent dilemma, "Doing it Right or Doing it Well, Which?" Creating a prayer book that speaks to contemporary Jews is an art, not a science, and we were humbled by the task.

Rosh HaShanah Morning Service

Hear the call of the shofar!

About the Division of the Shofar Service

Early on in the process of creating the machzor, the editors decided that, since the overall motif of Rosh HaShanah morning is the sounding of the shofar, we should consider spreading it out throughout the service.

Like synecdoche in literature, the symbol of the shofar stands for more than just a ram's horn. It represents the essential nature of the day. Indeed, it is more than the sound; it is the liturgy surrounding the shofar sounding. And more particularly, it is the themes of *Malchuyot* (sovereignty), *Zichronot* (remembrance), and *Shofarot*.

Long ago in its liturgical development, Reform Judaism did away with the Musaf Service on Rosh HaShanah (and everywhere else), but kept the practice of the three shofar sections. The editors of *Mishkan HaNefesh* thought that the sounding of the shofar, and its attendant liturgical themes, could be developed and dramatized more powerfully by placing the three sections into three different places in the worship service, each positioned in some logical place. After experimenting during the pilot program, we settled on the following: *Malchuyot* would come in the *Amidah*, following the *m'loch* declaration. *Zichronot* would follow the scriptural readings, including God's remembering Sarah and Hannah. And *Shofarot* would precede the closing prayers and the redemptive message of the second part of the *Aleinu*, *l'takein olam b'malchut Shaddai*.

Spreading out the sounding of the shofar in this way allows the congregation to spend more time with each theme. *Chevruta*, musical selections, mini-sermons—much can be innovated.

The Challenge of Choosing Wisely
Using *Mishkan HaNefesh* can provide worship leaders with a challenge. This is not because it restricts choice—quite the contrary! Rather, it is because there are so many choices. Each service leader has to make wise choices that will engage and inspire his or her own community.

Or not. The choice is up to the worship leaders. One could even decide to feature the three sections one after the other, as in *Gates of Repentance*. (See also the discussion by Rabbi Janet Marder on the shofar liturgy, below, page 75.)

In addition to the three formal shofar sections, the shofar can also be sounded earlier in the service, as well as on the evening of Rosh HaShanah. These are moments when it is possible to once again focus on the prime imagery of the day. In keeping with the overall approach of *Mishkan HaNefesh*, the idea is not to do everything. Rather, it is to decide what matters most for you and your congregation and employ the machzor in that endeavor.

MORNING BLESSINGS / *BIRCHOT HASHACHAR*
Pages 113–119: Study Texts

The study texts featured here range from the biblical to the modern period. Included on page 116 is the *locus classicus* for the imagery of the different books on the New Year. For a more modern take on this image, see the observation from Rabbi Maurice Davis on page 45 of the machzor.

SONGS OF PRAISE / *P'SUKEI D'ZIMRA*
Pages 130–135: Psalms of Praise

The selection of psalms presented here is limited, due to the fact that many congregations—especially those with multiple services—abbreviate this portion of the service. We wanted to include a selection from Psalm 27, based on its light imagery and association with the Days of Awe season.

Pages 136–137: A Taste of the Shofar

In addition to the three appearances of the shofar in the Morning Service, we have placed an optional sounding here—something like a musical motif that anticipates far greater development later on in the performance. A sublinear commentary on page 137

Graphic Imagery
Note the graphic of the Hebrew word *shofar*. This is a way of helping to provide some thematic visual imagery to indicate distinct sections throughout the machzor. We use a similar graphic with the *K'dushat HaShem* section that follows, as well as in several other places.

is provided especially for those who wish to combine the various shofar soundings.

About Cuts in the Liturgy
Yishtabach for Rosh HaShanah was shortened because of constraints in page layout and the length of the entire Rosh HaShanah service. This is the kind of painful decision that we simply felt was necessary for that particular service, which has so much in it. In general, we retrieved a great deal of language that had been excised from earlier American Reform prayer books—understanding that all the liturgy is poetry and metaphor, and that we no longer are restricted by the late nineteenth-century Reform criteria that prayer had to reflect what we believe with certainty in the most literal way, or be somehow verifiable. Robust commentary and an emphasis on expansive interpretation allows us to reclaim these classic words in new ways. That explains why twenty-first-century Reform Jews can say the words *Mashiach ben David avdecha* and mean by them a variety of understandings. But we also had to balance that new twenty-first-century hermeneutic with a respect for a certain American Reform *nusach* in other parts of the service, much of which is also determined by the music. It means that in the end, much of the traditional/ classic language was restored in this machzor, but not in every prayer.

Pages 138–140: *HaMelech*
Even though these words may be seen by some as sexist in nature, it was hard to justify not including them in the machzor. After all, the coronation of God as the Ruler of rulers (traditionally, King of kings) is difficult to ignore since the imagery is so essential to the day. Page 139 provides a corrective for those who prefer alternative theological images. *Mishkan HaNefesh* restores to the Reform Movement the traditional reading of the declaration as *HaMelech yosheiv*, invoking the immanence of God's majestic presence. The Shabbat version, which was used in *Gates of Repentance*, proclaims that God is *HaMelech HaYosheiv*, i.e., God is on the throne. But during the Days of Awe, the declaration without the second *"ha"* evokes a more immediate presence of God as Judge. To paraphrase the title of a wonderful book by the late Rabbi Alan Lew, this is real and we are completely unprepared.

SH'MA AND ITS BLESSINGS
Page 142: *Yotzeir Or*
The High Holy Day addition from Yose ben Yose has been restored here, suggesting once again the connection between light and spiritual

discovery. The words reflect a Talmudic teaching (*Chagigah* 12a) that the original light of creation (i.e., that which was created on the first day and not the fourth day) was too powerful for humans and therefore was hidden away, to be discovered only by the righteous. Presumably this ancient insight was seen as too recondite for earlier Reform liturgy. We included it, in part, because of the general identity between light and spiritual awareness. Indeed, "the numinous is luminous."

Pages 148–149: *Ahavah Rabbah*

These pages are illustrative of our decision to weave Zionism, *Ahavat Tziyon*, and Israel into the fabric of the machzor. Two other obvious examples are: the *Ahavat Tziyon* section of *Minchah* and the prayer for the state of Israel (p. 275) that speaks of "Zionists and Zion's friends in all countries."

Pages 150–159: *K'riat Sh'ma*

For congregations that wish to read the entire *Sh'ma*, the traditional second paragraph can be found on page 154. Another theological approach is presented on page 155. See also the notes to pages 26–31.

Pages 162–163: *Redemption*

These two pages present a clear example of integrated theology. The faithful translation on the right is balanced by a theology of human adequacy on the left.

HAT'FILAH

Pages 172–182: *Untaneh Tokef*

It is hard to find a more provocative piece of High Holy Day theology than this ancient *siluk* that served to introduce the *K'dushah*. It calls to mind Robert Kennedy's phrase, borrowed from the ancient Greek, "the awful grace of God." We could not omit this declaration from the machzor, but neither could we present it unadorned. What we did is offer the complete text, including the final lines, which are not found in *Gates of Repentance*. These lines are here because they serve to properly introduce the *K'dushah*.

We did not provide the allusions to Rabbi Amnon of Mayence familiar to us from the previous machzor, which are historically suspect, but we did offer variant theologies and perspectives. (See the discussion by Rabbi Janet Marder on counter-texts, below, page 72.) We also strove to focus on the unavoidable message of the day, in part echoed by Carl Sandburg's poem "Limited" (p. 181). On the one hand, we knew that many people come to services on the High Holy Days and wish to be chastened into accepting the uncertainty of life. On the other hand, we wished to eschew the theology that posits that bad things happen to people because they deserve it.

Page 186–191: *Uvchein*

On these three paragraphs, please see the notes above to pages 48–52.

Pages 199–207: *Shofar: Malchuyot*

After piloting this movement of the shofar service earlier in the day, we settled on positioning *Malchuyot* in the *T'filah*—pinned, as it were, to the *m'loch* declaration in the *K'dushat HaYom*. Interestingly, *Gates of Repentance* similarly placed a distinct liturgical rubric inside the *T'filah* on Yom Kippur, namely the *S'lichot* prayers. (*Mishkan HaNefesh* presents them as a separate rubric.) There is further precedent for this placement of *Malchuyot* as well, namely that historically it was located within the *T'filah* section of the *Musaf* service.

As stated at the start of this chapter, by splitting up the Shofar Service we hoped to enable congregations to spend more time with each of its themes, examining them in greater depth.

Each section of the shofar presentations begins with the basic text from the Talmud (*Rosh HaShanah* 34b), listing the three themes of the shofar sounding. Each section ends with *Areshet S'fateinu*. In this way we framed the similarities of the three sections.

Starting Point

The Midrash envisions the angels asking, "When is Rosh HaShanah? When does the New Year begin?" The answer is found not on the calendar but in our deeds: when we recognize the humanity and the divinity within every human being and act accordingly. (*Deuteronomy Rabbah* 2.14)

Page 201 offers the *piyut V'ye·eta·yu*, as well as a modern rendition of "All the World Shall Come to Serve Thee." *Gates of Repentance* placed this *piyut* in the midst of the Yom Kippur Afternoon Service, but in this machzor we editors wanted to restore it to its traditional place. It is a new translation of the Hebrew prayer, which can be sung to the classical melody by Joseph Friedlander. Our new translation emphasizes universalism over the historic triumphalism of "All the World. . . ." (Note the universalistic theme of the last stanza, "When all people sing together. . . .") As the late Reform lay leader Larry Kaufman once blogged, there is still a place in Reform Judaism for the aspiration of universal harmony. In many ways, Reform Judaism has moved beyond "All the World Shall Come to Serve Thee"—that is to say, we rarely sing English hymns anymore, and the archaic English of the poem is not what we are used to. But the message of this old standby remains important: Jews of all stripes would do well to remember that we are here to make the world a better place. We serve God by daring still to hope for a world that will get better, because we believe we are created by God, the One our tradition calls the King of kings and therefore able to make a difference.

Page 214: *Shalom*

The traditional reference to the priests has been restored in this prayer. The point was not to return to the elitism or hierarchy of our priestly past but rather to acknowledge the prayer's historical context. We were cognizant of the musical settings that this change necessitates. We believed, however, that a liturgical remembrance of a priestly tradition (and contemporary observance in other denominations) merited this inclusion, as the recent statement of Reform Jewish Responsa attests. (See sidebar.) In short, we wished to honor a very important aspect of our communal

From CCAR Responsum 5771.4—
Priestly and Levitical Status in Reform Judaism
To say that priestly *yichus* (inherited status) is irrelevant to our religious life should not suggest that the awareness of priestly status has completely disappeared from among our people. Reform Jews can and often do acknowledge the fact of their yichus as a matter of family tradition. They will often maintain the title *HaKohen* or *HaLevi* in their Jewish names, as testimony that they were born to a father of either status. We certainly have no objection to this custom. We would emphasize, however, that when Reform Jews do recognize their priestly or levitical descent, they express thereby a sense of connection to historical institutions rooted in our Biblical heritage and not to some (non-existent) Reform version of those institutions.

past. This is especially timely during the period leading up to Yom Kippur, when traditionally the High Priest symbolized the national hope for expiation and atonement.

Page 221: Prayer of the Heart

An innovation within this machzor is the posing of questions to the individual worshiper. Such material can of course also be used in *chevruta* and as *chomer lidrosh*.

Pages 222–225: *Avinu Malkeinu*

See the notes above to RH pages 74–77. (On the theology behind our presentation of this prayer, see the discussion by Rabbi Elaine Zecher, below, page 115.)

READING OF THE TORAH / *K'RIAT HATORAH*
Pages 226–229

The editors knew that much wonderful material could not be included in the book. After all, the traditional machzor alone would be far too long, coupled with the tremendous amount of new sources that we included. Therefore cuts to the traditional *matbei·a t'filah* had to be made. Some are small, but everything adds up. This explains why there are no *Ki Mitziyon* and *Baruch Shenatan* verses in the Torah presentation.

We retain the Thirteen *Midot*, an integral part of the High Holy Day message, and we have included the *nora* addition to the *Sh'ma* here.

Pages 232–235: Various Blessings

There are a number of opportunities to connect the public Torah reading with personal events (the *nefesh* of the *Mishkan*), including *gomeil*, *simchah* events, and the honor of saying the blessing over the Torah. See also the various blessings for healing that follow the reading of Torah.

Pages 236–243: Torah Readings (also pages 330–335)

From its inception, *Mishkan HaNefesh* sought to honor the legacy of *Gates of Repentance* while also acknowledging the potency of the traditional machzor. At the same time, we were also open to new possibilities in scriptural readings. The result—which is aided by having two volumes—is a plethora of choices.

For Rosh HaShanah we have presented four possible Torah readings. They are: the traditional Reform selection of Genesis 22, the newer Reform option of Genesis 1 (which first made its appearance in *Gates of Repentance*), and two other texts not previously included within a Reform machzor: the traditional Genesis 21, and Genesis 18. Rabbi Lawrence Hoffman, in his wonderful commentary *Gates of Understanding 2*, relates the reasons for including Genesis 1: it offered an alternative text for those not comfortable with the *Akeidah* (binding of Isaac) and, moreover, it reflects the New Year's identification with the creation of the world. Genesis 21 was restored here because we feel its key message of God remembering Sarah is an integral component of the Days of Awe. We were also aware that the treatment of Hagar and Ishmael at the hands of our ancestors will cry out *darsheini* to many of us and to our congregants (see example on facing page).

As a corrective to Abraham's ostensible allegiance to God over his own family, we have also offered Genesis 18, wherein God is challenged by Abraham. There is some disagreement in modern as well as ancient sources concerning the notion that God is being taught by Abraham. (After all, it is God who initiates the conversation.) Nevertheless, the editors saw this chapter as a text that can be more readily interpreted in favor of the actions of Abraham. We wanted our heroes in the Bible to act with moral grandeur and spiritual audacity (to cite Heschel) and, when it comes to Abraham, this is as close as it gets.

Piloting of the machzor convinced us not to add too much *chomer lidrosh* in the blue pages and sublinear comments. We are confident that worship leaders will find years of teaching and preaching possibilities with these new texts.

On page 243, the additional verses of chapter 22 constitute for Dr. Norman Cohen (offered in a lecture) an "eleventh trial" of Abraham. Abraham is the pioneer who gives up home and security to receive the blessings of greatness and also of countless descendants. Ironically it is his brother, Nahor, who stays home and enjoys manifold blessings of many children. *Darsheini!*

Pages 248–261: Haftarah Readings

We include the four readings from *Gates of Repentance*. The First Samuel material makes a lot more sense now that Genesis 21 is included. Verse 19 on page 251 actually includes God *remembering* Hannah. This verse provides a logical anchor for the shofar section that follows.

Pages 262–269: Shofar: Zichronot

Throughout, *Mishkan HaNefesh* minimizes its instructions to the congregation. You will not see directions like "please rise." Even the frequent use of italics on these pages should not be construed as responsive reading invitations. In general, italics are used for scriptural verses.

In the interest of saving space, the Hebrew is not included here. Nevertheless, the Hebrew texts of many of these verses lend themselves to musical renditions, such as *Zacharti Lach* on the middle of page 265.

Pages 270–275: Community Blessings

We offer a number of innovations, such as the French section of the prayer for Canada (p. 273). In addition, the Prayer for Our Congregation (p. 270) expresses gratitude for those who support the Jewish community, and for all members of our community—even though they may not be Jewish.

On Hagar and Ishmael Today (Genesis 21)

> Pack your loads on my back. / Force me to your destination. / I will go the
> mile you demand, and even a mile further. / With your guns and your au-
> thority / you can force me to do your will, / but never can you take away
> my freedom, / for that lies deep within my soul / where your bullets and
> harsh words / can never reach. / No load is as heavy / as submitting to
> slavery, / and that load I will never bear.
> —NYEIN CHAN, *a refugee living in a camp in Myanmar (Burma)*

Mishkan HaNefesh includes Torah passages that may be otherwise un-
known to some Reform Jews. Genesis 21 is restored to its traditional place
as a Torah reading on Rosh HaShanah. This passage is sure to launch a lot
of sermons and provoke some controversy. After all, its main subject is the
expulsion (some say: emancipation) of Hagar, the Egyptian handmaiden
to Sarah and mother to Abraham's son, Ishmael. Ishmael is also expelled
(or: emancipated). They almost die.

As Mother Teresa once observed, "Being unwanted, unloved, uncared
for, forgotten by everybody, I think that is a much greater hunger, a much
greater poverty than the person who has nothing to eat. . . . Loneliness is
the most terrible poverty." These words resonate with the text of Genesis 21. We also need not be speaking of harsh wilderness conditions. The
civilized world is harsh enough.

Think about the "Ishmaels" in many countries and their forced exile
from the world they know. While many American students go abroad
to study for a semester or two, many more students come to the Unit-
ed States from other countries to take advantage of the wider range of
educational opportunities offered here than in their own country. Every
year, for example, some 800,000 Chinese students study abroad. With
the Chinese government's one-child-per-family laws (repealed in 2015),
that means that many families are sending off their one-and-only son or
daughter to a foreign country for several years, not just a semester.

The anxiety of being so far away must be very difficult for the mothers.

Of course, the worry that mothers feel for their children is not the only
emotion that drives the story of Hagar and Sarah in Genesis 21. Initially it

is understandable for us to see Sarah's actions as harsh and Hagar's plight to be a grave injustice. Still, the writer of Genesis doesn't seem to see it that way.

By the time we get to this narrative, we know that Isaac, Abraham's son through Sarah, is going to be the child through whom God's covenant promise would be realized (Genesis 17:21). Sarah had tried to circumvent further delay by having Abraham sleep with Hagar in hopes of finally having an heir.

When Hagar conceives, though, the slave-woman treats her mistress "with contempt" (16:4). Even though Hagar is a slave and a subordinate wife to Abraham, her pregnancy gives her status over Sarah in her barrenness. Sarah responds harshly, and Hagar runs away into the desert, returning only after God has made a covenant with her about her son. There is a high anxiety level here, even as it is clear that both women want to protect their children (16:5–15).

When Isaac at last is born to Sarah, the conflict between the mothers reaches its climax. Sarah will tolerate no competition for her son's rightful inheritance, and Abraham cannot bring himself to disagree. Though Ishmael is, indeed, the firstborn son of Abraham, the preferential order of rank is given to the firstborn son of the primary wife (21:10–11). Sarah's demand that Hagar be expelled distresses Abraham, but God reminds him that this is part of the covenant plan (v. 12). God will fulfill a covenant through Ishmael as well, making "a nation of him also" (v. 13).

And yet, one can't help but feel the pain in the story. As Sarah's nest goes from empty to full, as she moves from a state of barrenness to abundance, from cold to hot, Hagar's nest has gone from hot to cold. Death seems to await Hagar and Ishmael.

Walking the desert with her son on her shoulder, Hagar reminds us of the news reports of refugee mothers fleeing war-torn countries, clutching their frightened children. We see Hagar when we read of a young and pregnant runaway, lost and alone. We know the stories of women who have had to raise their children in a world that, in spite of the prosperity of so many, still does not know how to care for the people on the margins.

Fortunately, the God of Genesis did not forget Hagar. She wandered in the desert with her son, rationing the water that was left and giving most if not all of it to her son (v. 15). When it was all gone, she laid him under a bush, hoping for just a little shade, a little comfort before he died of thirst. She separated herself "at a distance" from the boy because she could not bear to watch him die, could not stand to hear him calling for her and having nothing to give him.

We then read that "God heard the boy's voice," and God's messenger spoke to Hagar: "Do not be afraid. . . . Stand up. Lift the boy, and hold strongly onto him with your hand—for I will make of him a great nation" (vv. 17–18). God then put a well of water in the middle of the desert and put hope for abundance in the midst of desperate circumstances.

The cries of these mothers are well known to God. The question is: are they heard by those of us?

Being unwanted, unloved, uncared for, forgotten by everybody, I think that is a much greater hunger, a much greater poverty than the person who has nothing to eat. . . . Loneliness is the most terrible poverty.

Pages 278–285: Shofar: Shofarot

The editors did not want to suggest when one should deliver a sermon but—as the customary place has tended to be following the prayers for the country and State of Israel—it might make sense to split the second and third shofar sections with a sermon or teaching. We placed this section in anticipation of the conclusion of the service and the hope that worshipers will leave the service with the sound of the shofar in their ears and the idea of *tikkun olam / tikkun midot* in their hearts.

CONCLUDING PRAYERS

Pages 286–299: Concluding Prayers

Page 294 offers a musical piece in addition to the more traditional closing songs. Page 301 offers the chance to include the *chatimah* theme for the first time, anticipating the days to come. Some may choose to sound the shofar at this point, as well.

(On counter-texts for *Aleinu*, see the discussion by Rabbi Janet Marder, below, pp. 72–73. On closing songs, see the discussion by Cantor Evan Kent, below, p. 119.)

Rosh HaShanah Afternoon Service

Tashlich

We did not include a *Tashlich* service in this machzor, as it seems unlikely that people will want to take these books to the waterside. We also did not include a pre-Rosh HaShanah *S'lichot* service. Both of these services will be made available separately.

Pages 304–327

We included a brief afternoon service for those congregations who choose to pray this liturgy, perhaps before *Tashlich*. The innovations presented here are the same as those in the Rosh HaShanah morning service.

Yom Kippur Evening Service

I forgive, as you have asked.

The motif of the evening service, beyond its obvious connection with *Kol Nidrei*, is a verse from the Book of Numbers in which God accepts the forgiveness of the recalcitrant Israelites. The idea is that forgiveness from God is a given. Therefore the drama of Yom Kippur lies not in the question of whether or not God will be compassionate, but in whether or not *we* will be compassionate with ourselves and with each other, even as we submit our entire selves for review.

Pages 2–3: The Tallit
Since it is customary on Yom Kippur—unlike during the rest of the year—to don a tallit for the Evening Service, we included the prayer for doing so. We also provided a prayer for those who do not wear a tallit. Our aim was to provide a spiritual moment for both kinds of worshipers: those who wear the tallit and those who do not—instead of excluding those who do not wear the tallit from this page of the machzor.

Page 8: Candlelighting
For those who kindle a memorial candle at home, we have created a blessing and a reading.

Pages 10–13: *T'filah Zakah*
We favored an explicit recognition of the five different physical acts from which we abstain on Yom Kippur. In keeping with our ongoing attempt at welcome and inclusion, we also provided here a spiritual meditation for those who are unable to avoid eating or drinking.

An obvious marker that this is not our grandparents' Reform High Holy Day prayer book is our inclusion of a modified *T'filah Zakah* (pp. 12–13), previously omitted from the Reform liturgical tradition. In this prayer the worshiper enumerates and connects their sins with various acts and asks for forgiveness. Additionally, the person forgives any who have caused them pain or harmed them. This prayer was popularized by R. Avraham Danzig, in his *Chayei Adam* (eighteenth century). (See also the discussion by Rabbi Leon Morris, below, p. 98.)

Pages 14–21: *Seder Kol Nidrei*

We move from singular atonement to communal. Following the *Kol Nidrei* declaration we included the statement of forgiveness on page 20. The point of Yom Kippur is not to convince a judgmental Deity to pardon us, so much as it is our acceptance of a loving and compassionate God, already offering forgiveness. The work of the day, then, is not asking for forgiveness, but instead planning out a course of repentance and renewal. (See also the discussion by Rabbi Janet Marder on countertexts, below, p. 73.)

Although intrigued by the traditional inclusion of the *Shehecheyanu* after *Kol Nidrei* (there is a nice balance between Rosh HaShanah's *Kiddush*, followed by the *Shehecheyanu*, and *Kol Nidrei*—i.e., the "*Kiddush*" for Yom Kippur, followed by the *Shehecheyanu*), we decided its appearance here would confuse more than edify the worshiper, so it is not featured.

SH'MA AND ITS BLESSINGS
Pages 28–29: *Sh'ma*

The typeface used for *Baruch Shem* is the same size here as that of the *Sh'ma*, reflecting the notion that on Yom Kippur, we are like the angels who chant these words continually. Throughout the year, *Baruch Shem* is said softly, probably because it is non-biblical and less sacred than the *Sh'ma* itself. On Yom Kippur, we recall the so-

Midrash Deuteronomy Rabbah 2.36
Another explanation: *Listen, Israel* (Deut. 6:4). The Rabbis say: When Moses ascended to heaven, he heard the ministering angels saying to God, "Blessed is God's glorious majesty forever and ever." This [declaration] Moses brought down to Israel. And why does Israel not make this declaration publicly [i.e., aloud]? Rabbi Assi replied: This can be compared to a man who stole jewelry from the royal palace, which he then gave to his wife, telling her, "Do not wear these in public, but only in the house." But on the Day of Atonement—when Israel are as pure as the ministering angels— they do recite publicly, "Blessed is God's glorious majesty forever and ever."

lemnity with which the people responded when the High Priest uttered the ineffable name of God. The *Shulchan Aruch* (*Orach Chayim* 319.2) states that we should say the *Baruch Shem* line aloud. Midrash *Deuteronomy Rabbah* 2.36 teaches that on Yom Kippur we resemble angels, so we are therefore allowed to say aloud the sentence said by the angels (see sidebar on previous page). See also the notes above to RH pp. 26–31.

HAT'FILAH
Page 66: M'chal
The mirror of Rosh HaShanah's *M'loch*, *M'chal* suggests a kind of transposition of the letters, hence reflecting the balance between God's sovereignty and desire to forgive. The two actions are completely different and yet strongly related: to act like a king, with the authority and right to judge, and to forgive. The art is in finding the right balance.

VIDUI
Unlike *Gates of Repentance*, *Mishkan HaNefesh* removes the Confession and Forgiveness sections from the Amidah and places them in their own rubric. Even now, at the beginning of Yom Kippur, the list of sins will be balanced through acknowledging the goodness we have practiced and our capacity for performing mitzvot in the future.

Pages 82–84: Short Confession
Here, and throughout the book when this phrase appears, we have restored the Hebrew to say that we *are* insolent (*anu azei fanim*), instead of the usual denial (*she·ein . . .*). This version is attested to in *Seder Rav Amram* (ninth century) and was later changed. We have restored this earlier version, which serves as a simple declaration of the gap between who we are and where we need to grow. The traditional rendering appears to be some kind of superstitious refusal to state the obvious. We rejected that approach and have chosen to use this earlier, more honest version.

Throughout the confessions on Yom Kippur, we have presented various ways in English to help the community in the work of repentance—in spite of the challenges of doing so, due to our often thick defense systems.

Pages 86–95: Long Confession

This machzor's *Al Cheit* lists differ from one service to another. The editors thought about grouping them based on subject matter (such as gossip). Instead we opted for a structure designed to speak to each individual soul through the medium of communal language. (On the theme of this evening's *Al Cheit* list, see Rabbi Janet Marder's essay, below, p. 70.) As a balance, page 93 offers a more positive statement about our capacity for righteousness.

S'LICHOT

Pages 96–111

We have seized upon *Sh'ma Koleinu* as a central text for the *S'lichot* services on Yom Kippur. It appears in some services more than once, in some cases as an ongoing refrain. Other innovations include the presence on page 99 of the poem by Rachel, tied into the notion of God hearing our voice when we cry out. We also included the Thirteen *Midot* as a way of recognizing its core message of compassion.

During the *S'lichot* section we presented the Thirteen *Midot* (Attributes) with a refrain (p. 107), showing the gap between our shortcomings and God's benevolence: "We are insolent . . . but You are the essence of mercy." (On the Thirteen *Midot*, see also the discussion by Rabbi Leon Morris, below, p. 97.)

The contemporary *piyut* on page 108, written by Rabbi Sheldon Marder, is built around a phrase from a medieval poem by Rabbi Yehudah Halevi, "If I could see God's face within my heart." Like a garden, we are always a work in progress, and we need to be tender toward each other and ourselves as we continue to grow and develop.

During the creation of *Mishkan HaNefesh*, the editors came to understand that tearing oneself apart with remorse and guilt does not necessarily lead to a better, more repentant self. Yes, an honest assessment and recognition of moral failing must occur; but there should also be compassion for, and understanding of, imperfection.

Page 112–115: *Avinu Malkeinu*

See the notes above to RH pages 74–77. (See also the discussion by Rabbi Janet Marder on counter-texts, below, p. 72.)

Do Not Adjust Your Machzor—
or, the Goldschmidt Variations

As *Mishkan HaNefesh* takes its place as the new machzor, it is natural that some of the differences between its Hebrew text and that of *Gates of Repentance* will confuse some readers. They are not mistakes.

For instance, *Gates of Repentance* includes the declaration *HaMelech hayosheiv* shortly before the *Bar'chu*. Ironically, such words are found also in the Shabbat liturgy. The more appropriate rendering for the Days of Awe is *HaMelech yosheiv*. There is something more immediate about this declaration. It reminds me of the title of a book about the Days of Awe by Rabbi Alan Lew (ל″ז), *This Is Real and You Are Completely Unprepared*. So *Mishkan HaNefesh* restores this more traditional statement, dropping the second definite article (*ha-*); see the sublinear note there (RH 138).

Another change deals with the words said at the beginning of the *Vidui* on Yom Kippur: "we are accustomed to asking God for forgiveness, although we are not stiff-necked enough to deny our culpability." This makes no sense. It's like observing that "You can't have your cake and eat it too." Of course you can! The proper statement is, "You can't eat your cake and have it too." Likewise, the declaration should be: "We *are* so stiff-necked." That's why we are in need of forgiveness. Hence, the Hebrew now reads *Anu azei fanim* and not *She·ein anachnu azei fanim*. We have removed the illogical *ein* ("not").

Our correction actually reflects the version in the ninth-century *Seder Rav Amram*. The original version there says, "We are in fact so stiff-necked as to maintain that we are righteous and have not sinned, but we have sinned." In other words, we are actually so arrogant as to want to maintain the fiction of being perfectly righteous and never sinning; but actually, we really have sinned. It then follows naturally that we should confess.

Rabbi Lawrence Hoffman, a great source of help on matters such as this gap between logic and our received tradition, suspects the additional word, *ein*, crept in over time because people were hesitant to say that we are indeed all that arrogant. They preferred saying "we are not so arrogant" as to maintain that we have not sinned.

The editors and proofreaders consulted many different *machzorim*, noting variants in the text. In many cases, the editors of *Mishkan HaNefesh* followed the Goldschmidt version of the traditional machzor when there have been questions of the best text to use. Ernst Daniel Goldschmidt (1895–1972) was a liturgical scholar who created what are considered authoritative critical editions of liturgical texts, including the machzor for the High Holy Days. These changes may also cause some confusion for readers of *Mishkan HaNefesh*, especially in relation to *Gates of Repentance*. Each of these choices reflected the desire on the part of the editors to render the most faithful version of the tradition.

So, back to mistakes. Yes, there surely are some mistakes in *Mishkan HaNefesh*. We used some of the top, most thorough Hebrew-English proofreaders in the country. Even so, the new machzor is a human endeavor and, as such, it is necessarily imperfect. As with every book, we will correct mistakes that we become aware of in subsequent printings. But much of what might at first glance seem like a mistake is in fact a careful, intentional choice.

Yom Kippur Morning Service

You stand this day, all of you, in the presence of Adonai your God.

The motif of this service, taken from the traditional Reform Torah reading for the morning, speaks of standing before God. It draws on the theme of the renewal of the covenant as well as imagery of standing in judgment. Beyond the image is the continuation of the Torah reading and its vital message: repentance is not too far from us.

MORNING BLESSINGS / *BIRCHOT HASHACHAR*
Page 137: Individual Preparation
We included the recognition, as we did in the Evening Service, that some are not able to fast.

Pages 156–157: *Asher Yatzar*
On the juxtaposed poem by May Sarton, see the discussion by Rabbi Sheldon Marder, below, page 110.

SH'MA AND ITS BLESSINGS
Page 178: *Yotzeir Or*
Added to the usual Reform version of this blessing are words that prefigure the gates of *N'ilah*, as well as light references related to hope and goodness.

Pages 186–187: *Sh'ma*
Once again—for Yom Kippur only—the *Baruch Shem* is printed in the same size typeface as the *Sh'ma* itself. See notes above to pages 28–29.

Page 196–197: *Mi Chamocha*
See the discussion by Rabbi Janet Marder on counter-texts, below, page 72.

HAT'FILAH

Pages 206–216: *Untaneh Tokef*

See the notes above to RH 172–182. (See also the discussion by Rabbi Janet Marder on counter-texts, below, p. 72.)

Pages 222–227: *Uvchein*

On these three passages, please see the notes above to RH pages 48–52. On the phrase *tz'michat keren l'David* (p. 224), see the discussion by Rabbi Sheldon Marder, below, page 88.

Pages 252–253: *Avinu Malkeinu*

Once again, the Janowski version is preserved intact (see above, notes to RH pp. 74–77). It begins with the list of pleas. Unlike in *Gates of Repentance* but in line with traditional liturgy, here *Avinu Malkeinu* precedes the Torah service.

READING OF THE TORAH / *K'RIAT HATORAH*

Pages 264–270: Torah Readings (also pages 331–339)

It is up to the worship leader to decide which of the four Torah passages is to be read, at both the Morning and Afternoon Services. The four choices include the Reform legacy piece "You stand this day . . ." from Deuteronomy, as well as another Reform legacy piece from Leviticus 19. We also included a little bit about the holy day from Leviticus 16. Moreover, *Mishkan HaNefesh* adds verses from Deuteronomy not found in *Gates of Repentance*. The theology of 30:1–11 might be considered troublesome, which perhaps is why these verses were not included there. The *Mishkan HaNefesh* editors liked the repeated use of the word *shuvah* and its connection to the overall theme of the day.

In addition, two narratives are included that are linked to the themes of Yom Kippur. Genesis 4, featuring Cain and Abel, offers the basic insight that we all have the choice to do the right thing. Robert Fulghum argues that the Hebrew at the end of verse 7 is the most important word for us to remember: *timshol*, we can *overcome* our urge to sin.[1] This first act of human violence invites the reader to ponder the nature of

---

1. Robert Fulghum, *Maybe, Maybe Not* (New York: Ivy, 1993), pp. 1–4.

human aggression. Another midrashic interpretation suggests that Cain repented of his sin, which thus provides plenty of *chomer lidrosh* on the subject of repentance.[2]

Another option for Torah reading is the story of Joseph and his brothers, which appears on pages 332–333 in the Minchah Service. Some may find that this reading, with its emphasis on reconciliation and forgiveness, works well on Yom Kippur morning. On this reading, see below, in the commentary about those pages.

We believed that these links, although external to the Torah, allowed us to introduce new narratives that may be read on Yom Kippur.

Pages 275–283: Haftarah
We presented a haftarah blessing on page 279 that is different from the blessing in *Gates of Repentance*. This first version is more traditional and offers themes such as messianic hope and a more peaceful Zion. The second, shorter version on page 280 is the more familiar Reform blessing from *Gates of Repentance*.

Pages 284–289: Community Blessings
See the notes above to RH 270–275. One innovation in this service, opposite the Prayer for the State of Israel, is a "counter-text" on page 289. Ehud Manor's "I Have No Other Country" represents a challenge to the State to always live by its sacred values.

Page 284: Prayer for Our Congregation
This innovative new prayer reflects the especially inclusive nature of Reform Judaism and focuses on the value of community-building.

VIDUI USLICHOT
Pages 292–317
For Yom Kippur morning, we have placed these two rubrics together as one section. *Sh'ma Koleinu* is a prominent motif, and an expanded litany of communal and personal faults is also included. As with the evening

---

2. See, among others, *Midrash Tanchuma*, Solomon Buber, ed. (New York: Sefer, 1946), vol. 1, p. 19.

before, there are also prayers of recognition of the good we have done.

On the personal *cheshbon hanefesh* worksheet (pp. 308–309), see Rabbi Janet Marder's essay, below, page 71.

Page 303: On New Year's Day

Hebrew poetry is used throughout *Mishkan HaNefesh* as modern *piyutim*. This poem by Yehuda Amichai is an example. (On this topic, see Rabbi Sheldon Marder's essay, below, page 101.) The use of modern Hebrew poetry stands alongside environmentalism and Zionism as a distinct and pervasive theme of this machzor.

CONCLUDING PRAYERS
Pages 318–319

Yom Kippur morning prayers do not end in any substantial way. The worship continues throughout the day. Nevertheless we provide a few readings and a musical selection for those looking for some kind of "closing" ritual.

Yom Kippur Afternoon Service

You shall be holy.

With the afternoon service, *Mishkan HaNefesh* takes a radical departure from *Gates of Repentance*. For one, we have dispensed with the *Avodah* section, from Creation to Redemption, though a different kind of *Avodah* service begins on page 443. Our *Minchah* service features the Torah and haftarah readings, restored to their traditional place at the beginning of the service, and an expanded *T'filah* that features seven ethical virtues, *midot*, as a focus of our preparation toward repentance and renewal. Finally, there is a *Vidui Uslichot* section and concluding prayers. The overarching theme is *tikkun midot hanefesh*. (On this service, see also the discussion by Rabbi Janet Marder, below, p. 77.)

READING OF THE TORAH / *K'RIAT HATORAH*
We placed the Torah and haftarah readings back at the beginning of the service, as was done historically, not only because that is the traditional place, but also due to the strong themes of righteousness and repentance that they present. Far more than an additional bit of inspiration, they frame the day's task. Hence, having them at the beginning makes sense.

Pages 332–333
The Torah readings have been described above (see the notes to the Morning Service). As noted there, the story of Joseph and his brothers from Genesis 50 is presented as an option here. Many themes are at play, from the rapprochement between the characters to the brothers' lies— arguably, for the sake of *sh'lom bayit*. Although there is no actual connection between the Joseph saga and Yom Kippur (nor, for that matter, is there one with Cain and Abel), the ancient postbiblical sources posit a connection. The Talmud (*Rosh HaShanah* 10b) teaches us that Joseph was freed from his Egyptian prison cell on Rosh HaShanah; and the

Book of Jubilees (chapter 34) teaches that the brothers cast Joseph into the pit on Yom Kippur. This text also reflects the ancient idea that the legend of the martyrdom of ancient rabbis, which is historically recited on Yom Kippur, is in atonement for the sin of the brothers—kidnapping Joseph and selling him as a slave. The editors rejected this theology, but we found the story of reconciliation fitting for Yom Kippur.

Pages 341–350: Haftarah
Jonah, the haftarah, is presented here in its entirety, including the prayer of Jonah from chapter 2. We also include the selection from Micah that is traditional for Yom Kippur afternoon (and *Tashlich*).

HAT'FILAH
Page 354: *Midot HaNefesh*
This page explains the thinking behind the *Midot HaNefesh* material that is interspersed throughout the *Amidah*. The editors envisioned that each year congregations will choose to focus on a particular *midah* throughout the service, or perhaps in a study session before or after. The intention was not that all the *midot* would be covered every year.

Page 405
On the poem "Face," see Rabbi Sheldon Marder's essay, below, page 108.

The Editors' Approach to the Latter Part of Yom Kippur

This chapter and the following one provides insight into the various services that *Mishkan HaNefesh* offers for worship during Yom Kippur afternoon. It will be up to the service leaders to determine their specific plan for the day. Most likely, many options will be offered in alternating years—something like a triennial cycle, perhaps.

The approach to Yom Kippur afternoon used in *Mishkan HaNefesh* was to offer various choices for helping congregants experience a meaningful day. We also wanted to provide material that could be presented without a large budgetary commitment in terms of music or theatrical enhancements, though such things are certainly wonderful if they are possible.

Minchah and *Eileh Ezk'rah* are intended to complement each other, focusing on the themes of *tikkun midot* and *tikkun olam*. On this interplay, see Rabbi Janet Marder's essay, below, page 65.

Yom Kippur *Avodah* through *N'ilah*

Yom Kippur *Avodah* Service:
May we ascend toward the holy.

This service is a completely new creation, modeled on fifteen steps toward
holiness. The fifteen steps reflect the
stairs leading to the southern wall
entrance of the ancient Temple in
Jerusalem, and they are also related
both to the steps in the Temple and to
the fifteen Songs of Ascent in the book
of Psalms (as explained by Rabbi Janet
Marder, below, pp. 78–79). Complete
explanations of the service are found
within *Mishkan HaNefesh* itself.

Distinctive Layout
This service and the following ones,
until *N'ilah*, eschew the two-page
spread that is favored in the rest of
Mishkan HaNefesh. Each of these
services has unique features that the
editors thought were better served
with a linear layout. Moreover, these
services are original, creative liturgies
that are not based on a historic
liturgical structure, and therefore the
right side/left side interplay would
not work for these services.

The editors sought to create a meaningful experience of reflection,
prayer, poetry, and music that could be offered on Yom Kippur afternoon
without a big budget for a costly production. (A common complaint
about the *Avodah* service in *Gates of Repentance* was that, in order to
"stage" it properly, a large production budget is required.) Congregations
may choose to read all fifteen steps, or favor just a few each year. We
also hope that, in the future, new music will be written for some of these
pieces, for both the Hebrew and English.

(On this service, see also the discussions by Rabbi Janet Marder and
by Rabbi Leon Morris, below, pp. 78 and 98, respectively.)

Eileh Ezk'rah:
For these things I weep.

This service is a complete departure from the historic Yom Kippur mar-
tyrology. The introduction on page 516 of *Mishkan HaNefesh* explains

the new approach. It is important to note that the ten contemporary people commemorated in the new *Eileh Ezk'rah* are not martyrs. The last paragraph of the introduction on page 516 explains: "We remember them today not as martyrs and not as saints, but as human beings defined by their moral choices, their sacrifices, their sense of responsibility. Theirs are stories of repairing the world: *tikkun olam.*"

The question has been raised that including Shmuel Zygelboym sends a message that suicide is sanctioned. Certainly by including Zygelboym we opened up a discussion about moral choices and a conflict of values. What is our approach to the teaching of Masada and those who died *Al Kiddush HaShem* during the Crusades? As Rabbi Sheldon Marder has noted, Zygelboym embodies spiritual resistance for the sake of saving the Jewish people. Our inclusion of him in the service certainly is not meant to say that suicide is praiseworthy, but only that one man at one moment made a profound moral choice that surely took into consideration the issue of suicide.

In general, those chosen for this list represent Jews who lived—and died—in adherence to their Jewish values. (One of the ten was not Jewish; he lived out values in keeping with those of Judaism.) Their lives ended tragically but their stories continue to inspire. They are modern enough for us to identify with their having the courage of their convictions. (See also the discussion by Rabbi Janet Marder on this service, below, page 79.)

Yizkor:

These are the lights that guide us . . . These are the ways we remember.
The service of memory, *Yizkor* (from the Hebrew root meaning "remember"), has been a traditional component of Yom Kippur observance since antiquity. The earliest source for *Yizkor* may be found in Midrash *Tanchuma* (see sidebar on next page), which cites the custom on Yom Kippur of recalling loved ones who have since departed and pledging charity on their behalf. Since the Torah reading on the last day of the pilgrimage festivals (the holidays of Sukkot, Passover, and Shavuot, when the ancient Israelites made a pilgrimage to Jerusalem) mentions the importance of donations—"let no one appear before God empty-handed" —*Yizkor* was added to these holiday services as well. (See also the dis-

cussion by Rabbi Janet Marder, p. 80.)

Like the other Yom Kippur afternoon material, this service, too, has a completely new framework in this machzor. Pages 538–539 explain the approach. There are seven ways to reflect on loss and memory, grief and healing. They are presented in a linear style but with the understanding that actual grief does not come in such an orderly fashion. Pages 568–569, although not marked with folios, provide a graphic depiction of the various relationships we hold dear and, because we hold them dear, make us vulnerable to loss and grief.

> **On the Importance of Donations**
> We read in Midrash *Tanchuma* (*Haazinu* 1): "Atone for Your people, Israel, whom You have redeemed" (Deuteronomy 21:8)—*Kapeir l'am'cha Yisrael* (the first clause) refers to the living; *asher padita* (the second clause) refers to the dead. This comes to teach us that the dead require redemption by means of the living. Therefore, our practice is to remember the deceased on Yom Kippur by pledging charity on their behalf.

Some congregations may choose to light a seven-branched menorah for the service.

For those who will go directly from *Yizkor* to *N'ilah*, we provided a verse from Song of Songs (p. 607) that ties the theme of love being stronger than death with *N'ilah*'s theme of "sealing."

N'ilah:

You hold out Your hand.

The final service contains, beyond the usual theme of closing gates, an image of God's outstretched hand, yearning to meet us in our journey toward repentance. This text, *Atah notein yad*, will be repeated throughout the service as a message of hope. (See also the discussion by Rabbi Leon Morris, below, p. 98. On the absence of an *Al Cheit* confessional in this service, see Rabbi Janet Marder's essay, below, p. 70.) We included here another recognition that not all are able to fast and yet their observance of Yom Kippur is just as valued.

This service features the traditional liturgical switch from "inscription" (*k'tivah*) to "seal" (*chatimah*).

The editors of the machzor envisioned a *N'ilah* service that would capture the imagery of time running out for repentance (i.e., the closing gates), while at the same time expressing relief that God anxiously desires our return—hence, "You hold out Your hand." We wanted people to leave the synagogue uplifted, inspired to make the coming year one of more goodness.

Therefore, we added on page 659 a *Hakarat Hatov*—a litany of good deeds that we have performed in the year gone by. On page 660 we are instructed to go forth in gladness, to rejoice in the renewed opportunities for righteousness and holiness. The concluding tone of the service should be one of joy and uplift.

Part 2
Essays

The New Reform Machzor Is a Solution, but What Is the Problem?

Rabbi Edwin Goldberg

The following essay was written during an early stage in the creation of Mishkan HaNefesh. *It asks the question: What exactly would a successful new prayer book do that had not been done before? It is printed here in order to provide insight into the process of creating* Mishkan HaNefesh.

Introduction

Harvard professor Clayton Christensen likes to tell the story of the fast food chain that found that about half of milkshake sales occurred in the morning. These buyers came into the restaurant by themselves, bought a milkshake and nothing else, and drove away with the milkshake rather than consuming it at the restaurant. Looking deeper, researchers learned that the buyers were commuters, and the job of the milkshake was to provide distraction on a long commute and to tide them over until lunch. For this job, the milkshake competed with bananas, donuts, breakfast bars, and coffee. Commuters bought milkshakes over the competition because milkshakes take a long time to consume, don't slosh or leave crumbs, and can be held in one hand or be put into a cup holder during the drive.

Most of us don't think of milkshakes as a solution to a problem (i.e., hunger, boredom, need for convenience). But it turns out they *are* a solution, and happy is the fast food establishment that knows the problem its product seeks to address.

With a big *l'havdil*, this insight has been at the forefront of the thinking that guided the editorial team of the new machzor. We were not creating a book, per se, so much as a sacred tool that is part of the solution to a problem (or set of problems). Therefore, before any decisions could be made concerning the book itself, we needed to make sure we accurately understood the problem. After all, as the late Stephen Covey used to teach, it doesn't matter how efficient you are at chopping down trees if you are actually in the wrong forest.

So before creating the book as a team, the rabbis on the editorial committee spent a number of months devising a vision statement (see below). This statement, crafted by Rabbi Sheldon Marder, reflects not only our proposed solution in the form of a sacred book, but also the challenges such a book sought to address (with the understanding that the book itself could only be a part of a larger pool of worship perspectives.)

A Vision Statement for a New Reform Machzor, 2009

T'shuvah is the chief goal of the Yamim Noraim, and a machzor is our indispensable manual and guide. We aim to create a machzor that will serve Reform Jews as they seek repentance, new direction, and a sense of return to God and the Jewish people.

We envision a twenty-first-century machzor that . . .

- provides meaningful liturgy to those who pray regularly, and welcomes those who are new to Jewish spirituality and practice;
- inspires Reform Jews to participate in the multifaceted experience of the *Yamim Noraim*—from feelings of awe to moments of solace, from the solitude of contemplation to the solidarity of song and worship;
- draws from the deep wellsprings of Jewish liturgy, history, thought, music, interpretation, and creativity;
- guides worshipers, in accessible ways, through the journey of *t'shuvah* and *cheshbon hanefesh*;
- values continuity and incorporates the outlook of the twenty-first-century Reform Jewish community of North America;
- bridges the personal and the communal, the ritual and the ethical dimensions of the *Yamim Noraim*.

We embrace the rich liturgical voices of the Jewish past and the aspirations of our people today. Among those aspirations is the wish for a machzor whose words, tone, and theological range are uplifting, inviting, and challenging. We seek metaphors and images of God that will speak to our time, as the prayers of *Union Prayer Book II* and *Gates of Repentance* spoke with depth and authenticity to theirs. We seek an integration of tradition and innovation, prayer and music, speech and silence, the struggle with God and the struggle with being human.

Most important to our work are the people for whom this book is intended: the members of a dynamic, ever-changing, and diverse Reform Movement who gather in community to experience awe and forgiveness and hope. Some call themselves classical Reform; some seek to recover and reinterpret the broader Jewish heritage. Traditional views of God resonate with some; others find it hard to believe in God at all. One can hardly overstate the challenge before us, as we strive for a liturgical message that illuminates and inspires.

We are open to exploring the use of early *piyutim* and modern poetry, visual art used as text, commentary that is intellectually engaging and spiritually provocative, music that we already cherish as well as musical innovation. We will attempt to frame with sensitivity texts that are painful or disturbing. Translations and original materials must be beautiful and evocative, conveying to worshipers an appreciation of our inherited liturgical tradition, as well as Judaism's relevance to their lives. We seek a balance between the creative retrieval of classical texts and the present-day sensibilities of Reform Jews.

Mishkan T'filah is our base text, and a great deal will flow from the structure it provides. At the same time, the historical machzor is central to our efforts, as it has been to Reform liturgists of the past. Our work will be informed by the various *minhagim* developed by Jews over many centuries in response to their circumstances and their faith.

What do we mean by "base text"? *Mishkan T'filah* provides us with fundamental principles and a carefully crafted framework and design. The specific requirements of a machzor may lead us to expand on *Mishkan T'filah*'s paradigm, but our plan is to create a book that is a fitting companion to *Mishkan T'filah*.

Mishkan T'filah's right side/left side format encourages diversity, choice, and the inclusion of many "voices"; the use of counter-text; and a stimulating balance of *keva* and *kavanah*. It allows for midrashic creativity and the presentation of different ideas about God, in order to reflect contemporary realities of Reform Judaism and the Jewish world. The dialogue—or confrontation—between the two facing pages also seems particularly suited to the themes of *s'lichot*, *t'shuvah*, and *cheshbon hanefesh*, which are fundamentally relational and dynamic in nature.

We will take seriously the diverse opinions about gendered language for God. Ours will be more than a superficial "He said, She said" approach; gender is far more profound and complex than substituting one noun or pronoun for another. We look forward to an exploration of gender that leads Reform Jews to encounter and experience God in interesting, meaningful ways.

The Editorial Core Team will oversee a process involving diverse working groups of rabbis (assigned to such tasks as translation, commentary, and poetry); consultation with cantors and educators to assure that music and learning are integral to the book; consultation with academic experts in relevant fields; and responders who will evaluate our work and offer critique. Self-evaluation will be ongoing. We are committed to creating an efficient review and piloting process that will result in the timely production of the book.

We believe the Reform nature of this machzor will be most evident in its respectful yet fresh approach to tradition; in its unwavering commitment to the equality of men and women; in its attention to the present-day concerns, fears, and hopes of the people who will pray from its pages; in its faithfulness to the ethical dimension of Judaism; in its embrace of the universal and the particular; and perhaps, most of all, in its effort to deal with the tension between the historical theology of the High Holy Days (God's sovereignty and judgment) and more contemporary beliefs, such as the "theology of human adequacy."

We are mindful that the High Holy Days are a time of change and challenge for each person; yet also, profoundly, a time of memory—a time when a familiar smell, sound, or *taam* can make all the difference for many of us; and a time when families and communities take stock and grow closer. We take seriously the feelings associated with holiness, as we envision a machzor that encourages and activates these significant levels of experience.

What follows are my comments regarding what I believe to be the most salient points of the statement.

COMMENTARY

T'shuvah is the chief goal of the *Yamim Noraim*, and a machzor is our indispensable manual and guide.

In designing a machzor we find it helpful to begin with the end in mind, another useful insight from the late Stephen Covey. Specifically: What do we hope for worshipers to have realized by the end of *N'ilah*? How will their lives have changed? What will be different? The simple answer is to suggest that *t'shuvah* will have occurred, but what does this mean? Certainly it seems impossible to measure the inner life of a person, so would we even know if we had succeeded? Such is the work of rabbis—that we will never know for sure if the experiences we provide lead to the results we desire. Nevertheless, even if we cannot know for certain where people end up, we most assuredly should design the best "map" possible. Hence our machzor will be designed to lead the worshiper through a process that we label the "i-axis," in which the various services build up to a climax where painful truths are realized, change is considered and adopted, and the individual leaves with a plan for self-improvement.

We seek metaphors and images of God that will speak to our time, as the prayers of *Union Prayer Book II* and *Gates of Repentance* spoke with depth and authenticity to theirs.

During the course of our work, we will consider the various Friday night services in the *Gates of Prayer* and how each one reflects a different theology. Then there is the integrated theology of *Mishkan T'filah*. Our approach is to build on the integrated theology while at the same time understanding that, to put it mildly, the theological "stakes" are higher on these Days of Awe. In other words, on a given Friday night one might very well focus on a non-dualistic image of God, or perhaps the theology of human adequacy, and *zei gezunt*. The High Holy Days cannot be treated in the same manner. Somewhere, a more traditional theology of hierarchy has to be offered if we are to be true to the essential message and tone of these days. Therefore we know that the greatest challenge of the book most likely will be how to reflect this tradition, while at the same time not turning off all those who cannot reconcile such views with the God in which they want to believe.

I call this the "Singing in the Rain" factor. The popular song was eventually slated to be a movie. Asked about it, its future star, Gene Kelly, said he had no idea what the movie would be about but he was sure of two things: "There will be rain and I will be singing in it." We know as editors that there is going to be some form of *Untaneh Tokef* in the book, even if during our investigation we discovered how relatively minor this *piyut* (actually a *siluk*) was in its initial incarnation. In addition to the more traditional approach to God, we will offer—especially on the left side of the two-page spread—various images of God that challenge the hierarchical model, especially making use of poetry and well-chosen metaphor.

Most important to our work are the people for whom this book is intended: the members of a dynamic, ever-changing and diverse Reform Movement who gather in community to experience awe and forgiveness and hope. Beginning with the end in mind is not only about what we want the worshiper to experience by *N'ilah*. It is also about making sure we understood who that worshiper is and who the worshiper is not. In this case, although we value the prayer experience of the rabbi and cantor, we are clear in our desire to fashion a prayer book for *amcha*. In other words, we are the first to admit that the book will not be the most user-friendly option out there. As with *Mishkan T'filah*, it is highly likely that the clergy who use this book initially will find it less enjoyable than the congregants they serve, simply because it requires significant preparation to use it well. We know that the book would take plenty of forethought and would call upon a balance between offering directions and allowing the congregation to have their own experience. No one said that leading effective worship should be easy, and we believe that the goal is not to offer simple worship. Having said that, we want worship that is complex rather than complicated, and we will strive to meet that goal as best we can.

Conclusion

Creating a new machzor for the Reform Movement is a daunting task, and we are humbled by the challenge. Nevertheless, we are guided by a clear vision of what we wish to produce, as well as aided by the outstanding work of those who prepared earlier *machzorim* and siddurim. Shortly after beginning work on the machzor, I came across an original 1895 *Union Prayer Book II*, with my great-grandfather's name inscribed inside. I enjoy imagining Lewis Wessel praying with this book at Shaaray Tefila on the Upper East Side. Our new book will be quite different, of course, but if we succeed, it will seek to solve the same essential problem: How do we help ourselves return to our sacred path, in a world that continually seduces us away from the work that we must do?

Praying in Captivity:
Liturgical Innovation in *Mishkan Hanefesh*

Rabbi Janet R. Marder

Said Rabbi Eliezer: One who makes one's prayer keva (*set,*
fixed), that person's prayer is not true supplication.
—Mishnah *B'rachot* 4:4

What is meant by [making one's prayer] kcva? *Rabbi*
Jacob bar Idi said in the name of Rabbi Oshaiah: One
whose prayer seems like a heavy burden. The Rabbis say:
Whoever does not say it in the manner of supplication.
Rabbah and Rabbi Joseph say: Whoever is unable to add
something new. —Talmud *B'rachot* 29b

Rabbi Abahu said in the name of Rabbi Eleazar: [The
meaning is] one should not recite prayers as if one were
reading a letter. Rabbi Aha said in the name of Rabbi Yose:
[The meaning is] one must add something new each day.
—Jerusalem Talmud *B'rachot* 4:4

I invite you to think about ways you might introduce
risk to safety, mystery to the familiar, and novelty to the
enduring. —Esther Perel, *Mating in Captivity*

In an interview in *The Sun Magazine*, psychotherapist Esther Perel
speaks of the extraordinary pressures put on married couples these
days, given two equally strong human needs and the difficulty of satis-
fying both in a long-term marriage. She comments: "Our demands are
contradictory: Give me predictability; give me surprise. Give me comfort;
give me life on the edge. Give me familiarity; give me novelty." These
formidable expectations of marriage, she adds, are unprecedented in the
history of the institution. "A passionate relationship in which we ask for
novelty and mystery from the same person we look to for security and
stability—that is a grand new invention in the history of humankind."

Her exploration of this dilemma, entitled *Mating in Captivity*, sets out to discover whether passion can survive within the constraints of the marital relationship.

A similar tension between these two contradictory human needs—familiarity and novelty—surfaces in our Sages' discussion of prayer. Prayers with fixed times, structure, format, and content make communal worship possible; link Jews across time and space; imbue prayer with a specific set of shared concepts and values. Perhaps most important is the sense of comfort and belonging evoked by words and melodies ingrained in our memory. Yet reciting the same prayers three times a day may soon devolve into mechanical, mindless mumbling. Hence the Sages' dual desires for the fixed and the fluid, the received texts enlivened by elements of novelty added each time we pray.

Mishkan HaNefesh employs innovation as a source of freshness and novelty—a way to de-familiarize the familiar, awaken mind and spirit, and lead to a more reflective reading of traditional prayers. Even more significant is the hope that innovation will be a catalyst for deeper personal connection with the themes and concerns of the High Holy Day liturgy.

What's new and different in *Mishkan HaNefesh*? This essay highlights categories of innovation, discusses the rationale for each, and examines the ways these changes can enliven the liturgical experience. (A comprehensive list of examples appears in the Indexes, which may be useful for those wishing to focus their teaching on a particular area.)

Time for Quiet Learning and Reflection

This machzor is constructed in a way that allows for a slower, more deliberate pace—one which integrates worship with thoughtful inquiry, learning, silent study or meditation, solitary introspection, and/or discussion. Commentaries appear on nearly every page, and study texts are placed throughout both volumes, highlighting major themes and liturgical units. Two services, *Avodah* and *Eileh Ezk'rah*, employ study material on almost every page; the Yom Kippur *Minchah* service includes a *T'filah* that is built around study and reflection. In some cases, special insertions encourage private meditation during cantorial solos. For example, *Mishkan HaNefesh* includes a "Personal *Hin'ni*" for silent reflection during the cantor's *Hin'ni* (RH 16). The machzor also provides sets of "Questions for Personal Reflection and/or Discussion" in several places (RH 221; YK 308–9; and throughout both the YK *Minchah T'filah* and the *Yizkor* service).

All these structural elements are designed to encourage worshipers to take time to think about the meaning of what they are saying. Rote repetition of familiar passages can be comforting; rhythmic chanting can alter consciousness; and both have their place in worship. But the supreme goal of the Days of Awe is personal transformation—a change in the way we live—and to achieve this, the intellect and heart must be deeply engaged.

Rather than moving through the liturgy in rapid, mechanical fashion, users of this book are prompted to reflect on theological and spiritual concerns and how they might relate to real life. In the same way that poetry forces the reader to slow down and pay attention to language, *Mishkan HaNefesh* aims to slow down the experience of worship to allow profound words and ideas to penetrate the mind and soul. The goal is a continual dialogue between the pray-er and the prayer.

A service structured to allow time for quiet study honors the intellectual as well as spiritual dimensions of worship, respects the freedom of individual worshipers to wander through the book guided by their own curiosity, and employs the power of silence to inspire heartfelt *cheshbon hanefesh*. In such a service, worship leaders may choose to "cover" less material in order to provide more depth and personal exploration.

Creative Reframing of Tradition: Wrestling with Big Ideas

Mishkan HaNefesh employs poetry, congregational readings, study texts, sublinear commentary, and even midrashim to interrogate and illuminate challenging religious ideas, including messianism, the afterlife and resurrection, Jewish chosenness, divine sovereignty and omnipotence, sin and forgiveness, and reward and punishment. Readings and commentaries seek not only to explain these concepts but to offer new and provocative interpretations—or, in some cases, direct challenges and alternatives.

Some of these innovations involve the recovery of traditional material previously excluded from Reform *machzorim*. For example, this machzor restores the second section of the *Sh'ma* (Deut. 11:13–21), eliminated in previous Reform prayer books because its theology seemed both logically and morally problematic, teaching that reward inevitably follows good behavior and that suffering is divine punishment for our misdeeds. *Mishkan HaNefesh* re-frames this section in a way that speaks powerfully to contemporary worshipers (RH 29, 154; YK 34, 190).

Noting that the second section of *Sh'ma* is addressed not to individuals but to the entire community of Israel (something that is clear in the Hebrew), the machzor argues that its theology is thus best understood in a communal context, rather than as a teaching about reward and punishment in the lives of individuals. Interpretive commentary relates this passage to environmental concerns and care for the earth—a larger theme that is reflected throughout the machzor. In this and many other instances, *Mishkan HaNefesh* encourages worshipers to adopt a more sophisticated, less literal reading of the traditional liturgy—one that allows its compelling message to remain relevant in our own time.

The editors were moved by Yehuda Amichai's poignant poem about the human desire to avoid difficult questions by removing problematic texts from the Bible—and from our life.

> I've filtered out of the Book of Esther the residue
> of vulgar joy, and out of the book of Jeremiah
> the howl of pain in the guts. And out of the
> Song of Songs the endless search for love,
> and out of the Book of Genesis the dreams
> and Cain, and out of Ecclesiastes
> the despair and out of the Book of Job—Job.
> And from what was left over I pasted for myself a new Bible.
> Now I live censored and pasted and limited and in peace ...[1]

This philosophy has often characterized the Reform Movement's approach to liturgy. We have historically censored or filtered out the difficult rather than retaining material that is intellectually, spiritually, or emotionally challenging. *Mishkan HaNefesh* has chosen a different path, allowing worshipers to grapple with these challenges and expand their

---

1. Yehuda Amichai, "*Hazman* ('Time') 29" from *Time* (New York: Harper and Row, 1979), p. 31.

interpretive capacities. This machzor aims at a deep encounter with difficult concepts, and more complex, rather than reductive, understandings of Judaism's "great ideas," with the goal of provoking a continual re-examination and development of these ideas.

Thus, for instance, *Mishkan HaNefesh* not only retains (and reinterprets) the phrase *David m'shichecha* (literally, "Your anointed one David"), but also expands the notion of messianism by drawing on contemporary Israeli and American poetry such as Rivka Miriam's "They Said Redemption Would Come" (YK 65), Ruth Brin's "Chosen People" (RH 81), and Lawrence Ferlinghetti's "I Am Waiting" (RH 289). These poetic works imbue abstract notions such as "redemption" and "salvation" with vivid, concrete, and emotionally rich content, encouraging worshipers to incorporate them into their own imaginative life.

So, too, *Mishkan HaNefesh* inspires fresh consideration of the traditional notions of resurrection and the afterlife in a multitude of ways: through commentary (for example, RH 47, sublinear); through contemporary readings such as "To awake from sleep each morning" (RH 123), "Where Does It End?" (YK 543), and "What Happens After Death?" (YK 577); and through literature ("Life After Death," RH 87; the passage from Willa Cather's "My Antonia," YK 560; and "Bright Mariner," YK 582). Beautiful and thought-provoking meditations introduce worshipers to many potential ways of understanding these concepts and finding inspiration in them.

Similarly, *Mishkan HaNefesh* grapples in serious fashion with the notion of sin. Recognizing the powerful valence, both negative and positive, attached to this term, *Mishkan HaNefesh* employs the word "sin" where it is appropriate, but also draws on a wider linguistic range to convey the nuances of improper behavior, including "wrongs," "failures," "misdeeds," "errors," "unethical acts," and "thoughtless, careless, heartless actions." The phrase *Al cheit shechatanu l'fanecha* is translated not as the literal "The sin we have sinned before You," but in more nuanced fashion, as "The ways we have wronged You . . . and harm we have caused in Your world."

It is true that some worshipers find the word "sin" alienating, perhaps because the English word has Christian connotations. But the primary purpose of adopting broader terminology in this machzor is not to protect the sensibilities of worshipers or to minimize wrongdoing, but to reflect Jewish tradition more accurately—and to arrive at a more honest assessment of human misbehavior. The *Vidui* (Confession), after all, addresses comparatively minor wrongs committed in thought and speech, as well as heinous crimes such as sexual violence and murder. Thus, the heavily-weighted terms "sin" and "iniquity" fail to capture the full range of behaviors addressed in the liturgy.

Careful readers can notice a more substantial engagement with "sin" in this machzor. *Mishkan HaNefesh* includes many more verses of *Al Cheit* (the Long Confession) than have been included in previous Reform prayer books—in some cases, for purposes of thematic resonance. For example, the list in the Yom Kippur Evening Service (pp. 86–87) highlights misdeeds related to speech, since that service includes the *Kol Nidrei*, which focuses on verbal commitments (vows) improperly undertaken or left unfulfilled.

This machzor also conveys an important spiritual progression, related to the issue of sin, which is found within the traditional liturgy but has not been included in previous Reform prayer books. The *N'ilah* service omits the *Al Cheit* litany of sins and emphasizes instead the liturgical phrase *Atah notein yad* ("You hold out Your hand"), thus highlighting the shift from self-abnegation to confidence in divine love and forgiveness.

But the purpose goes beyond a recovery of tradition. In *Mishkan HaNefesh*, traditional understandings of sin are expanded, re-considered, and challenged—all with the goal of inspiring worshipers to engage in serious and unflinching examination of their own behavior. Recognizing that many of those in our pews have difficulty identifying with the traditional list of sins found in the *Vidui*, this machzor also offers a wide range of English readings, poems, and study texts to provoke renewed exploration of the themes of sin and *t'shuvah*, confession and forgiveness, as well as specific mention of sins with contemporary relevance (plagiarism, defeatist thinking, neglect of the body, etc.).

For examples of this kind of material, see: "To break the bonds of anger" (RH 33); the commentaries of Louis Newman and Rabbi Irving Greenberg (YK 85, 297); Rabbi Alan Cook's contemporary poetic reflection on the *Ashamnu* (YK 83); Yehuda Amichai's poem "On New Year's Day" (YK 303, including sublinear commentary); Robin Becker's

"Teshuvah" (YK 635), Dan Bellm's "Psalm" (YK 637); and the contemporary reading "Because I was angry . . ." (YK 293).

The full work of *t'shuvah* cannot be accomplished within the Day of Atonement itself; it requires many hours and entails personal encounters with those we have wronged. Nevertheless, *Mishkan HaNefesh* envisions Yom Kippur services in which substantial time is allocated for this inner work. Instead of the "all-purpose" confessional reading found in *Gates of Repentance*, this machzor includes a detailed, personal *cheshbon hanefesh* worksheet for sustained reflection by individuals or for paired dialogue (YK 308–309); and it includes several contemporary examples of confessions intended to inspire worshipers to create their own *vidui* (YK 299, 301, 305, 307).

A more striking innovation, perhaps, is the addition of confessional readings dealing with the issue of "recognizing the good" and self-forgiveness.

Readings on the theme of *Hakarat Hatov* draw attention to meritorious acts performed by the worshipers during the past year (YK 93, 312, 313, 424, 425, 659); another set of poems and readings centers on the theme of viewing ourselves as well as others with a compassionate gaze (YK 385, 581, 667).

These readings serve as a counterweight to the liturgy's intense focus on scrutiny of one's own wrongdoing. They also highlight a damaging moral failing—quite pervasive but usually not acknowledged in the prayer book: the inability to regard one's own behavior with the same gentleness and forgiveness we are expected to offer others. Most important, these readings seek to add an important, often neglected, dimension to the spiritual work of introspection. The goal of *cheshbon hanefesh* (moral inventory), after all, is not self-condemnation but an honest, realistic assessment of both our weaknesses and our strengths, our right and wrong actions. Chasidic teachers especially emphasize the importance of acknowledging the good within ourselves, noting that this is a spur to moral behavior—and helps prevent despair, apathy, and unwarranted self-abasement.

Counter-Texts

A significant innovation in *Mishkan HaNefesh* is the use of "counter-texts" that directly challenge the ideas presented in traditional prayers. Sometimes these counter-texts are recovered from the tradition itself; in other cases, the challenges are presented in a boldly contemporary idiom. These counter-texts often appear directly opposite the canonical prayers, making possible a dialogue between tradition and modernity, or between different voices within the tradition.

The dynamic interaction between two facing pages is intended to provoke deeper reflection—to help worshipers clarify their own beliefs and questions—and also to help them explore new ways of engaging with the liturgy. One can connect with a prayer, after all, not only by identifying with its sentiments but also by questioning, arguing, and offering alternatives.

For example, the reading "Who is like You among the silent?" (YK 197) presents a powerful counter-text for *Mi Chamocha*, in which the addition of a single Hebrew letter turns *eilim* (gods) to *il'mim* (the silent ones)—transforming a prayer in praise of God's redemptive power to a cry of anguish, denouncing God's silence in the face of human suffering. Its core idea is drawn from *Midrash M'chilta*; the sublinear commentary demonstrates that anger and protest were characteristics of medieval Hebrew religious poetry written during the time of the Crusades. Such material allows contemporary readers to see themselves within a larger historical pattern, and to find powerful language to voice their own grief and anger about God's silence during the Holocaust.

Two examples of counter-texts for the *Avinu Malkeinu* prayer are "Illumine for us the path of our life" (YK 112) and *"Avinu Malkeinu*: A Prayer of Protest" (YK 113). The first offers, instead of the traditional petitions to God, a series of questions directed at ourselves; in so doing, it avoids the temptation of placing responsibility for positive change on anyone but ourselves. The second reading questions the very existence of a compassionate Deity who hears our prayer.

Two examples of counter-texts for the *Untaneh Tokef* prayer are "I speak these words but I don't believe them" (RH 181), which explores our contemporary resistance to acknowledging our mortality, and "The Power of This Day" (YK 213), which challenges the liturgical declaration that "On Rosh HaShanah this is written; / on the Fast of Yom Kippur this is sealed: / How many will pass away from this world, / how many will be born into it. . . ." The latter reading seeks to re-capture the sense of awe and dread once evoked by the traditional prayer by re-framing its statements as questions instead: "Who will be missing when we gather next? . . ."

"Give us the strength to keep our promises" (YK 19) serves as a counter-text for *Kol Nidrei*, focusing not on the cancelation of vows but on summoning the resolve to fulfill difficult commitments—a moral imperative more appropriate to our own time. "Our calling is to praise the Living Source" (RH 287) serves as a contemporary counter-text for *Aleinu*, challenging the traditional prayer's notion of Jewish particularism, asserting instead that God "gives us a destiny shared with all human beings, and . . . binds our lives to theirs." This reading, and others throughout the book, articulates the universalistic theme that is inherent in the traditional liturgy for Rosh HaShanah, the day our Sages saw as celebrating the creation of the universe and of all humanity.

Theological Alternatives

One of this machzor's most striking innovations is its exploration of alternative theologies. Many readings in *Mishkan HaNefesh* challenge the traditional notion of divine omnipotence, focusing instead on human empowerment, our own responsibility for salvation. These readings are drawn from within the tradition as well as contemporary sources, demonstrating that Jewish tradition is not monolithic in its view of the human-divine partnership.

Examples of "human empowerment" readings drawn from the tradition include two teachings of Rabbi Levi Yitzchak of Berditchev ("In every action," RH 121 and "As the shadow follows the person," RH 177) and "The voice that redeems us / comes from within" (RH 163). Located opposite *MiMitzrayim g'altanu* (From Egypt You redeemed us), this reading builds on a midrashic source to question the notion of a redemptive power external to the human being. *Mishkan HaNefesh* also re-frames the liturgical phrase "*Atah notein yad*" (You hold out Your hand) as a reminder not only of divine compassion but of the human capacity to make positive change (YK 630, sublinear commentary).

Contemporary readings and commentaries emphasizing human empowerment include "Prayer is not something we do to God" (Rabbi Michael Gold, RH 175, sublinear); "Beloved Friend," a counter-text for *HaMelech* (Majestic God) (RH 139); "God's hands are our hands" (RH 25); and two poems by Ruth Brin: "When men were children" (YK 109) and "Letter to a Humanist" (YK 221).

Offered as counter-text to the traditional liturgy's celebration of divine sovereignty, several readings in *Mishkan HaNefesh* evoke a non-dualistic theology, in which God is not a separate entity "out there" but a Presence or energy inherent in all creation. Some of these readings are drawn from kabbalistic sources; others from contemporary literature; still others are original compositions, created for *Mishkan HaNefesh*.

A good example is "The Divine That Is Present Within and Among Us," a re-framing of *Avinu Malkeinu* (RH 224–25, including sublinear commentary). Rather than addressing an external entity, this prayer speaks of "The Power that passes through us and pervades all things," evoking a less hierarchical, but equally awe-inspiring sense of Divinity. Similarly, "*Sh'ma, Yisrael*—hear the voice of Channah" (RH 25) offers a non-dualistic interpretation of a phrase in Deuteronomy 4:35—*ein od milvado*—translated by JPS as "there is none beside Him," but read by Jewish mystics as "There is nothing but God." The Hebrew poet Zelda's "The Delicate Light of My Peace" (YK 496) and Walt Whitman's "Why! Who makes much of a miracle?" (RH 127) provide interesting literary examples of this mystical consciousness; the Yiddish "Dudele" of Rabbi Levi Yitzchak of Berditchev (YK 455–456) offers a Chasidic parallel.

Contemporary scientific concepts provide a fresh way of reading mystical texts about the all-pervasiveness of the Divine. For example, "Like an unbroken current," a re-framing of the *Yotzeir Or* prayer (YK 181), draws on a teaching of Rabbi Levi Yitzchak of Berditchev that the universe is animated by a continuous flow of divine energy, using the analogy of the flow of electric power. So also, "*Adonai Echad*: We Proclaim You One" (YK 185) draws on modern understandings of genetic and ecological relationships to convey a deeper understanding of the unity of all beings within God.

Changes in the Shofar Liturgy

One of the more controversial innovations in *Mishkan HaNefesh* was the editors' decision to break up the three sections of the shofar service (RH 199–207; 262–269; 278–285). In *Gates of Repentance*, the shofar service was placed at the very end of the Morning Service (traditionally it occurs in Musaf). Its three themes—*Malchuyot, Zichronot,* and *Shofarot*—were highly condensed and not clearly explained or related to the themes of the Days of Awe. Dividing the shofar liturgy in *Mishkan HaNefesh* allows for sustained attention to each theme and deeper explorations of the meaning of divine sovereignty, remembrance, and hope.

While there is no expectation that any Rosh HaShanah service will include all the material provided, the distinct placement of each section ensures that the three themes of the shofar liturgy can be clearly distinguished, and the wealth of material provided encourages a serious encounter with each theme. Each thematic section of the shofar service is introduced by a study text; each includes both traditional and contemporary readings on that theme; and each includes interpretive commentary to deepen understanding.

The placement of each section highlights its juxtaposition with other sections of the liturgy. For example, the "Sovereignty" section follows the *M'loch* prayer ("Reign over the infinite expanse of space and time"); the "Remembrance" section follows Torah and haftarah readings, all of which evoke sacred memories; the "Hope" section precedes *Aleinu*, focusing on a redemptive future. This expanded structure also allows for the inclusion of "*Kavanot*—Focusing Meditations for the Sounding of the Shofar" (RH 205). In addition, a new fourth section, "The Voice of Community" (RH 136–137) is introduced into the shofar liturgy to highlight an important contemporary source of holiness. For many Reform worshipers today, transcendent meaning comes not from the "vertical" connection with God but from the "horizontal" connection with others.

New Torah Portions Offered as Options along with Familiar Selections

Neither the *Union Prayer Book* (1945) nor *Gates of Repentance* (1978) included the traditional Torah reading for the first day of Rosh HaShanah, Genesis 21. *Mishkan HaNefesh* restores this reading and makes clear its relationship to Genesis 22, the traditional reading for the second day of

Rosh HaShanah (RH 236–239). In addition, *Mishkan HaNefesh* returns to tradition in restoring the concluding verses of Genesis 22, referring to the birth of Rebecca, Isaac's future wife (RH 243). Several completely new options for Torah reading are offered, as well: for Rosh HaShanah, Genesis 18 (RH 334–335); for Yom Kippur morning, Genesis 3–4 (YK 269–270); for Yom Kippur afternoon, Leviticus 16 (YK 334–337) and Genesis 50 (YK 331–333).

All of these additional options offer rich material for teaching, sermons, and reflection relevant to the themes of the Days of Awe. If prayer leaders want to retain the familiar readings on Rosh HaShanah and Yom Kippur, these additional readings may be fruitfully studied and discussed during Elul or the Ten Days of Repentance.

Congregational Readings based on Midrashim

Past Reform prayer books included many congregational readings composed of biblical verses, in keeping with that generation's focus on the Bible and rejection of the "legalism" of the Talmud. *Mishkan HaNefesh* offers Rabbinic literature as an additional source of spiritual meaning, in the hope that worshipers may grapple with—and perhaps internalize— some significant passages and concepts. It seeks to present midrashic material in a way that is accessible and inspiring, with relevance to contemporary concerns. In some cases the midrashim are offered almost verbatim, exposing Reform worshipers to the distinctive style of Rabbinic interpretation (for instance, "Faithful to the Covenant," YK 225). In other cases, midrashim provide the inspiration for contemporary readings that articulate Jewish values and teachings.

Out of a wealth of midrashim included in this machzor, two examples must suffice. First: "Coming Home: 'A Portion of Torah That Is Ours'" (RH 59), based on a passage in *Midrash Sifrei D'varim*, seeks to illuminate a phrase from the liturgy on the facing page: *v'tein chelkeinu b'Toratecha*, "may each of us find a portion of Torah that is ours." Using the characteristic Rabbinic strategy of parable, the midrashic reading explores the idea of Torah as the Jewish people's ancestral "portion." Our understanding of this concept is further expanded by a midrashic comment, found in the *Zohar* (YK 236, sublinear commentary), that each person possesses a unique letter of the Torah—a notion not to be taken literally, but one that conveys the sense that each individual can have a personal connection to this foundational Jewish text—and contribute unique insights and interpretations.

A second example: "Jacob had a dream" (YK 327), based on a midrash in *Pesikta d'Rav Kahana*, offers a contemporary reflection on spiritual inertia and apathy. It delves into the metaphoric meaning of "climbing Jacob's ladder" (seeking intellectual, moral, and spiritual growth) and relates it to the modern notion of process theology—an ever-evolving God. The midrash thus opens up a new way of understanding the human quest for self-improvement, seeing this striving for something better as a reflection of divine energy.

Readings Drawn from the Work of Modern Jewish Theologians

A central goal of the editors was to create a machzor that will be an educational text, continually enriching the Jewish learning of worshipers and whetting their appetite for further Jewish study. Theological works are a source of learning and inspiration—and an innovative one, for previous Reform prayer books do not draw extensively from such material. *Mishkan HaNefesh* offers worshipers an encounter with several significant modern Jewish thinkers, not only through study passages but through congregational readings composed of, or inspired by, their words.

These include Rabbi Leo Baeck (YK 435); Rabbi Eliezer Berkovits (YK 217, 489); Rabbi Eugene Borowitz (YK 449); Martin Buber (YK 434); Rabbi Abraham J. Heschel (YK 434, 460, 462, 491, 586); Rabbi Samson R. Hirsch (YK 501, 503); Rabbi Abraham Isaac Kook (RH 215; YK 31, 491); Franz Rosenzweig (YK 491); and Rabbi Harold Schulweis (RH 4; YK 561). The majority of worshipers will never have occasion to read the works of these thinkers in full, but *Mishkan HaNefesh* will increase familiarity with their names and some of their central ideas; and perhaps it will encourage some worshipers to seek out their writings.

A New Afternoon (*Minchah*) Service (YK 324–439)

The traditional *Minchah* for Yom Kippur is relatively brief, consisting of the reading of Torah and haftarah, *HaT'filah* (including *Vidui*/Confession), a series of *piyutim* (religious poems) and the Full Kaddish

(*Kaddish Shaleim*). *Mishkan HaNefesh* retains most of these traditional elements but offers a new and provocative theme for the afternoon of Yom Kippur—one that strongly resonates both with contemporary concerns and with the time-honored purpose of the holy day.

The heart of this newly-conceived *Minchah* service is a creative rendering of *HaT'filah*, based on the concept of *tikkun midot hanefesh* (repairing and strengthening the character, also known as Musar, or "working on oneself"). The seven blessings of the Festival *T'filah* are linked to seven Jewish virtues (*midot*), each of which is explored through study texts, congregational readings, and questions for reflection/discussion. Prayer leaders may choose to incorporate material from several *midot* in the service, or may prefer to focus on only one *midah* each year, perhaps supplemented by teaching and personal talks offered by clergy and congregants.

The Musar material presented in this service supports the work of introspection and *t'shuvah* that is central to the Day of Atonement—work that is ideally suited to Yom Kippur afternoon, a time when fewer worshipers are present, the atmosphere is more intimate and informal, and the pace is slower and more conducive to sustained reflection. All elements in the *Minchah* service—including musical selections, commentaries on the Torah and haftarah readings, concluding readings (YK 434–436), and the Rabbis' Kaddish (*Kaddish d'Rabanan*, YK 438–439, traditionally read after the study of sacred text)—reinforce the central theme of character improvement; all are intended to evoke a mood of profound soul-searching.

A New *Avodah* Service (YK 444–511)

The traditional *Avodah*, found in *Musaf*, consists of a narrative poem by Yose ben Yose (4th–5th centuries CE) recounting the history of Israel from Creation to the time of the Jerusalem Temple, with special attention to the Yom Kippur ritual performed by the High Priest on behalf of the people. While the Temple ritual must have offered ancient Israelites an intense experience of the power of holiness, its narrative description does little to engender a sense of holiness in contemporary worshipers. The *Avodah* service in *Mishkan HaNefesh* seeks a spiritual awakening by dramatically re-envisioning what holiness might mean in our lives today.

This *Avodah* incorporates the ancient ritual of Yom Kippur into a completely new framework: *Masa el Hak'dushah* (A Journey to Holiness).

It is framed by a statement of Rabbi Abraham J. Heschel—"Faith does not spring out of nothing. It comes with the discovery of the holy dimension of our existence" (YK 444 and 511)—and is structured around fifteen steps; a number drawn from the fifteen biblical Songs of Ascent as well as the fifteen steps leading up to the Jerusalem Temple. Ascent—the effort to rise higher in our spiritual and moral lives—is the central theme of this contemporary *Avodah*. (See the introductory material on pp. 445–447 and the "Fifteen Steps" reading on p. 450.)

Each step—each portal to holiness—is introduced by a brief excerpt from one of the Songs of Ascent (which could be set to music); each includes readings, poetry, study material, and a concluding blessing (some creative, some drawn from the tradition). As with the *Minchah* service, the prayer leader may choose to focus on just one or two steps in a given year, supplemented by teaching and personal talks, or perhaps on one of the four groups of steps (as shown on YK 452, 467, 477, 492). The overall movement is from the all-encompassing holiness of God (step one) to the human responsibility for holy work (step fifteen).

A New *"Eileh Ezk'rah* / These I Remember" (YK 516–533)

This service, traditionally included in the Additional (*Musaf*) prayers, recounts the story of the Ten Martyrs, rabbinic sages who were executed by the Romans in the first and second centuries CE. *Mishkan HaNefesh* includes a prayer in remembrance of these Sages (YK 516, 519), but it significantly reframes the *Eileh Ezk'rah* service around "Stories of Repairing the World" (*tikkun olam*). Thus, this service is a companion piece to the Afternoon (*Minchah*) service, which focuses on the inner work of character development. The partnership of *tikkun midot* and *tikkun olam*, twin foci of the Days of Awe, is made explicit in a reading by Rabbi Jan Katzew (YK 355).

The traditional *Eileh Ezk'rah* service centers on the notion of martyrdom for the sake of *Kiddush HaShem*—a concept that was deeply meaningful to Jews of the medieval period, when this service was created (see further YK 516). *Mishkan HaNefesh* rejects the glorification of martyrs and the romanticizing of suicide. It sets forth, as an alternative ideal, the giving of oneself in pursuit of justice, offering ten contemporary stories of heroic human beings who "gave their lives while struggling to right wrongs, make peace, and save others from humiliation, harm, or death." This service will educate Reform worshipers, familiarizing them with the deeds of figures who might otherwise be forgotten; it also offers strong support for the core Reform principle that we render highest service to God by rendering service to humanity.

A New *Yizkor* (YK 538–607)

The traditional *Yizkor* service, found at the end of *Shacharit*, is quite short: selected psalms; memorial prayers for the souls of loved ones, Jewish martyrs, and, in some versions, Holocaust victims and fallen soldiers; and *El Malei Rachamim* (God Full of Mercy). *Mishkan HaNefesh* presents a completely new structure for *Yizkor*, organized around the theme of seven memorial candles.

Drawing on the multifaceted symbolic associations evoked by light, the service takes mourners on a journey from raw grief through awareness of inner strength, remembrance, the cherishing of unique relationships, acceptance, gratitude, and peace. Each step includes music, psalms, a wealth of contemporary poetry, and reflections by traditional and modern writers. Each step concludes with a brief excerpt from Psalm 23 ("Healing Words"), questions for personal reflection, and a closing blessing. Service leaders may want to light a candle at each step, and to choose to read aloud a few of the many possible selections offered. Here, too, a given step may be highlighted by one or more personal talks given by clergy or congregants, with time allotted for silence.

This service acknowledges the complex emotional dynamics that many worshipers bring to *Yizkor*, offering prayers for those who mourn the suicide of a loved one (p. 558), a person who died by violence (p. 574), an infant or child (p. 573), or an abusive parent (p. 575). Rather than expressing a generalized sense of grief, most of the poems offer a unique and personal voice, reflecting on specific relationships (with a sibling, a spouse, a father or mother, a child, friend, or grandparent). A two-page spread following the Hana Senesh poem *"Yeish Kochavim"* (There are Stars, p. 567) evokes the panorama of human memories with a design suggesting stars in a deep blue sky.

Other novel elements of this *Yizkor* service: it includes four different translations/interpretations of Psalm 23 (pp. 594–595); diverse reflections on the afterlife (for example, pp. 541 and 583); prayers in memory of Jewish martyrs, and all people (not Jews alone) who were murdered in the Shoah (p. 599); a special prayer for the Righteous of the Nations (p. 600); and readings in memory of American and Israeli soldiers (pp. 600–601). *Mishkan HaNefesh* also restores the traditional reference to giving *tzedakah* in memory of a loved one (pp. 570–571; see the essay by Rabbi Margaret Moers Wenig, pp. xxviii–xxx).

For Those Who Struggle with Faith

Many members of Reform congregations define themselves as agnostics or atheists. Some, more comfortable with the language of science than that of theology, resist being asked to utter words they cannot believe. Yet something brings them to services on the Days of Awe—ethnic pride, family connection, love for the music, attachment to the community, inchoate yearnings, perhaps the desire for a meaningful connection with something greater than themselves.

Mishkan HaNefesh addresses the spiritual needs of those who struggle with traditional belief in several ways. Some readings are drawn from the writings of scientists who express their own spiritual longing, sense of wonder, or moral convictions. These words, by thinkers such as Carl Sagan, Richard Feynman, Lewis Thomas, and Ursula Goodenough, are placed in dialogue with the liturgy—a juxtaposition that conveys the clear message that science and religion may fruitfully co-exist. This machzor also includes contemporary poetry that celebrates the grandeur of creation in quasi-scientific language—works such as Alicia Ostriker's "molecular" cataloging of the wonders of nature (RH 171); Marilyn Nelson's meditation on the submicroscopic particles in dust (RH 213); and Jacqueline Osherow's inscription of sacred DNA in "God's Acrostic" (YK 495).

Other readings discuss the relationship of science and religion and the possibility of embracing both sorts of truth. Finally, many readings and poems directly articulate theological ambivalence, difficulty with prayer, anger, struggle, and the search for truth. A few examples must suffice: David Whyte's "Faith" (RH 65); Edward Hirsch's "I Was Never Able to

Pray" (RH 69); and a contemporary Israeli work, "The Mystery of the Necessity to Inform You" (YK 317).

The "Introduction to Closing Songs" (RH 93, 295) directly addresses dilemmas of faith, asking "Is it important that we believe everything we pray?" Such readings acknowledge and "normalize" questions and doubt, showing that they can comfortably coexist with moments of profound faith, catalyze spiritual development, and undergird a strong Jewish identity. *Mishkan HaNefesh* is a machzor that addresses seekers and skeptics as well as those whose faith is strong. The overarching goal, always, is to offer words that allow worshipers to articulate what they can honestly affirm and hold sacred.

Responding to the Realities of Our Community

The Yom Kippur Evening Service in *Mishkan HaNefesh* opens with a call for radical welcome and inclusion. "Let none be excluded from our community of prayer," it says. "Let all find a place in this sacred assembly." This machzor seeks to make this call real by directly acknowledging the diverse members of our Reform community, comprising a spectrum of religious observance and background, family structure, age, physical capability, sexual orientation, and gender identity. Rather than ignoring or denigrating those who (for a variety of reasons) do not follow traditional observances such as wearing the tallit or fasting, *Mishkan HaNefesh* seeks to open a door to spiritual meaning for these worshipers, as well (for instance, RH 106; YK 10, 132, 137, 324, 617).

Several readings in *Mishkan HaNefesh* acknowledge unpleasant but important realities in today's Jewish community, such as addiction, abuse, unemployment, betrayal, and adultery. Other readings deliberately include those who have sometimes been neglected or marginalized—including people with disabilities, those who are divorced, the elderly, caregivers, and transgender individuals. This machzor also acknowledges with gratitude the presence of non-Jews in our congregations, including family members and friends who gather with the community on the Days of Awe.

Finally, *Mishkan HaNefesh* takes note of a significant dimension in human life—our sexuality—that has not been directly addressed in previous Reform prayer books, but is a fundamental source of both joy and pain.

A notable addition, included for the first time in Reform High Holy Day liturgy, is *T'filah Zakah*, "A Prayer for Purity and Worthiness" (YK 12–13), a traditional prayer that frankly acknowledges human sexuality as a powerful instrument of healing or harm.

A New Approach to Gender

The most recent examples of Reform liturgy employ gender-neutral language, and for the most part, *Mishkan HaNefesh* follows suit. But a policy of strict gender-neutrality comes with a cost. Sometimes the effort to avoid linguistic offense results in language that is abstract, impersonal, and colorless. Therefore, *Mishkan HaNefesh* adopts instead a policy of "gender balance"—that is, it includes a few beautiful, spiritually evocative pieces that contain male or female language in reference to the Divine. These pieces were consciously chosen to avoid a preponderance of either male or female terms for God, recognizing the potentially harmful effects of such liturgical bias. The editors believe that the policy of gender balance demonstrates a kind of theological maturity for our Movement, suggesting that the Reform community can now accept all language for God as metaphorical and symbolic.

A New Focus on Israel

Mishkan HaNefesh is a consciously Zionist machzor, conveying the centrality of Israel to American Reform Judaism. It presents as liturgical texts at least fifty contemporary Israeli poems—more than any previous Reform prayer book—in most cases including the Hebrew originals as well as English translations. The inclusion of these works should serve to open American worshipers' eyes to the theological yearnings and struggles of our brothers and sisters in Israel. "Proto-Zionist" material is included, as well—that is, liturgical commentaries and traditional texts about the relationship between Jews in the Diaspora and the Land of Israel. The machzor also restores to Reform liturgy a significant number of traditional *piyutim* (religious poems), again, usually including the Hebrew text as well, to further worshipers' sense of connection with the Hebrew language.

   Mishkan HaNefesh is the first Reform prayer book to promote the traditional notion of *Ahavat Tziyon* (Love of Zion); it is one of the seven *midot* highlighted in the Yom Kippur Afternoon Service (pp. 392–393 and 394). In addition to the traditional prayer for the State of Israel, several contemporary prayers are included, some highlighting the concerns of Diaspora Jews; and some, like Ehud Manor's *"Ein Li Eretz Acheret"* (I Have No Other Country) conveying the notion that Israeli patriotism entails critique embedded in a framework of loyalty and love (RH 274–275; YK 288–289). The inclusion of creative Hebrew readings (with a new English translation) from *Kavvanat HaLev*, the siddur of the Israeli Movement for Progressive Judaism, such as Rabbi Mordechai Rotem's "Illumine for us the path of our life" (YK 112) also strengthens connections with Israeli Reform Judaism.

Additional focus on Israel comes from a new addition to the Yom Kippur Morning Service: a version of the traditional *Y'kum Purkan*, honoring all who teach Torah "in the Land of Israel and in the Diaspora" (YK 285). The *Yizkor* service includes a prayer in memory of "Those Who Fell on the Battlefields of Israel," as well as a contemporary poem by Yehuda Amichai about the experience of attending a memorial ceremony in Israel (YK 601). Finally, this machzor includes a creative re-framing of the notion of God's "return to Zion" (RH 209, sublinear commentary).

Conclusion: Praying in Captivity

Liturgical innovation is inherently destabilizing. Some worshipers and worship leaders will find it jarring to see familiar patterns disrupted, familiar ("traditional") words altered or missing entirely, and new readings that challenge or disturb their assumptions about appropriate prayer book language. But novelty and surprise can renew relationships and keep them alive. *Mishkan HaNefesh* was created with the belief that worshipers might find their relationships with God, Jewish tradition, and the community continually nourished by fresh perspectives and unexpected encounters. The disciplined structure of communal prayer is a gift offered to contemporary Jews by those who came before us. So also is the opportunity to explore that structure through the lens of modernity, with a gaze both loving and critical, attuned to the complexities of living as a Reform Jew in this time and place.

For an index of themes in Mishkan HaNefesh discussed in this essay, see below, pp. 131–34.

Translating Faith

Rabbi Sheldon Marder

Why Do We Make Prayer Books?

A mong all the languages of the world, there is only one that is truly foreign to most Jews: the language of faith. Although many of us learn to "get by" in one of its dialects, few of us ever become entirely fluent. That we stumble and stammer in this foreign tongue is not surprising; faith, after all, is a language that challenges us to describe the ineffable and comprehend the unknowable.

Perhaps the making of many prayer books is one result of the Jewish determination to master this most demanding of foreign languages—that we might give voice to our deep longings, high ideals, and noble aims. There is solace and inspiration in the belief that life has ultimate purpose; but the belief alone is not enough: we need words to explain it and a "spiritual grammar" to organize our elusive feelings about God.

Every translation of a canonical Hebrew prayer book is an attempt to grasp the language of Jewish faith—and make it our own. When we begin to sense that the language of our prayer book has drifted into the haze we call the past, we translate anew—proving once more that we hunger for holiness and for fresh and novel ways to make the prayers "sing," to bring forth their timeless beauty and their evocative power.

As for the new translations in *Mishkan HaNefesh*, our main goals were:

1. to reveal a prayer's essential ideas and qualities;
2. to make clear a prayer's core purpose, in relation to the real concerns of worshipers;
3. to make visible and audible in English the pervasive spiritual and poetic rhythm of the prayers—and to do so in theological and cultural terms that might overcome some of the obstacles to prayer (for example, diverse beliefs

about God and about the purpose of worship; and diverse
backgrounds and sensibilities among Reform Jews in
North America);

4. to offer to English-speaking worshipers prayers that
strive for the directness, the energy, and the aesthetics of
Hebrew prayer.

To these four goals let us add a series of bold metaphors framed by the
translators of the King James Version of the Bible (1611) to express their
vision of translating a holy book, and to which we shall return.

> Translation it is that openeth the window, to let in the light;
> that breaketh the shell, that we may eat the kernel; that
> putteth aside the curtain, that we may look into the most holy
> place; that removeth the cover of the well, that we may come
> by the water. (Miles Smith, prefatory essay to the Authorized
> Version).

Targum HaNefesh: All Prayer Is Translation

Nobel Prize recipient Octavio Paz (1914–1998) encourages us to think
broadly, expansively, and creatively about translation. "When we learn to
speak," writes Paz, "we are learning to translate."[1] In other words, from
birth to death, all human beings are translators: we turn our thoughts
and feelings, our hopes and disappointments, into language in order
to make our inner lives comprehensible to other human beings. We all
inherit a natural ability to translate the non-verbal into speech. Poets
and writers have a gift for translating the imagination into words; artists,
composers, and dancers translate reality into other modes of communi-
cation; and so on. How true to their original inspiration are these translations? To call them imperfect or flawed misses the point; for, in the
end, we can only *approximate* (through word, color, melody, or physical
movement) the original feeling or idea.

Thus Paz gives us a different way to think about the machzor's
"original" prayers. His insight helps us appreciate that all prayer—traditional Hebrew prayer, no less than its modern English counterpart—is a
translation. That is to say, it approximates a spiritual impulse even more

---

1. Octavio Paz, "Translation: Literature and Letters" (1971), in *Theories of Translation:
An Anthology of Essays from Dryden to Derrida*, ed. Rainer Schulte & John Biguenet
(Chicago: University of Chicago Press, 1992), pp. 152–62.

primal than the solid chain of Hebrew letters on the page. In a strikingly similar vein, the seventeenth-century metaphysical poet George Herbert (1593–1633) calls prayer "the soul in paraphrase"; or, as we find it in a Hebrew version by Shimon Sandbank: prayer is *targum hanefesh*—a translation of the soul.[2]

Faithful Translation

A felicitous metaphor comes to us from translator Edith Grossman (b. 1936).[3] She describes translation as "a living bridge between two realms of discourse, two realms of experience, and two sets of readers." For Grossman, a translation is a passageway between two worlds—for instance, the medieval world that produced, say, the Mourner's Kaddish and the far different world in which we pray it today. Most important: Grossman's notion of a living bridge implies that a translation should give us access to the world that generated the original text—as well as a glimpse of the experience of those who first used it.

Word-for-word (or so-called literal) translation holds out the promise that there can be a direct correspondence between languages (for example: the Hebrew word *g'ulah* means "redemption" in English, and *k'dushah* means "sanctification"). But literal translation misses the mark because languages differ strikingly in sound, syntax, rhythm, and structure; and, even more important, in the layered meanings of words and idioms that are unique to the culture in which a language grows.

A faithful translation presents idea for idea, feeling for feeling, and value for value—not word for word; and it resists the false premise of direct correspondence, asserting that we communicate the original text most accurately when its translation offers an *equivalent* way of saying the same thing—instead of purporting to offer an identical way. A faithful translation mirrors; it does not parrot.[4] The living bridge of faithful translation is assembled not from the nuts and bolts of lexicons and dictionaries alone. Rather, it is a complex span of "beams and struts":

---

2. George Herbert, "Prayer" in Shimon Sandbank, *Parallel Loves* (Jerusalem: Schocken, 1986), pp. 80–81.
3. Edith Grossman, *Why Translation Matters* (New Haven: Yale University Press, 2010), p. TK
4. Mark Hodes, based on comments made in personal correspondence.

history, theology, literature, and poetry—even art, music, the social sciences, and the "hard" sciences; all of these enrich the context and result in a more dynamic translation.

Let us turn to a discussion of two prayers in order to highlight the connection between translation and theology. Both are examples of prayer as "the soul in paraphrase"—*targum hanefesh*. Both appear in the series of blessings called *HaT'filah*, "Standing before God."

Prayer 1: "Give Your Believers a Basis for Faith"

The prayer to which we turn first—a High Holy Day insertion in *K'dushat HaShem* (Sanctification of God's Name)—helps us explore more deeply Grossman's notion of a "living bridge." In the traditional Hebrew text, and in the new translation (RH 50, 188, 314; YK 54, 224, 374), the prayer references the ancient Jewish tradition of King David as ancestor of the Messiah. Historically, Reform prayer books have omitted traditional references to King David as the ancestor of the Messiah, expressing instead a vision of a messianic age, created by human acts of *tikkun olam* (repairing the world). Indeed, *Gates of Prayer* includes the messianic song *"Eliyahu HaNavi"* in Havdalah, with the words *mashiach ben David* ("anointed one, son of David") in Hebrew and transliteration for singing—but there is no translation! In the Sanctification prayer in *Mishkan HaNefesh*, the Hebrew text, its transliteration, and the translation restore the traditional reference to David—but, as the translation makes clear, not as the literal progenitor of the Messiah, but as an emblematic figure who shines through Jewish history as a symbol of messianic hope.

The full text of this Hebrew prayer (*tz'michat keren l'David*), which now appears for the first time in a CCAR machzor, expresses the ancient belief that the radiance of David will someday "sprout forth"—a metaphor that links the image of light with the image of a growing plant to convey the idea that light will dawn gradually—in a slow, evolutionary process in which the darkness of ignorance and cruelty is transformed into the radiant glow of enlightenment and goodness. This notion of an evolutionary process ("May the sparks . . . soon grow bright enough for us to see . . . a promise of perfection") is faithful to longstanding Reform belief about the messianic age. The language of our new version of the Sanctification ("May the sparks of David . . .") demonstrates how translation can function as a living bridge between two worlds—or, put another way, as an intersection of tradition and innovation.

At first glance, the core of this prayer is something with which many Reform Jews readily identify: "Give Your believers a basis for faith." Closer inspection reveals more: the directness of the wording ("Give Your believers") replicates the directness of Hebrew prayer; and implicit in these words are two quintessentially Jewish ideas: (1) people we call believers also harbor doubts, and (2) the search for answers is never-ending. The confluence of tradition and modernity could make this translation one of the most challenging and also one of the most inviting paragraphs in the machzor. What's more, the cluster of images that constitute a basis for faith (true happiness for the Land of Israel, true joy in Jerusalem, David in relation to the experience of messianic hope) offers us the opportunity to "try on" a new language of faith—and thus grapple with authenticity, piety, and meaning as Reform Jews.

Prayer 2: "God Who Is Ours"

There are countless "correct" ways to translate every prayer. Let us look, for example, at a short section of *K'dushat HaYom* (The Holiness of the Day; RH 58, 208; YK 68, 236, 390). The opening phrase, "God who is ours"—used here instead of the more common introduction, "Our God and God of our ancestors"—replicates the Hebrew word *Eloheinu* in which God is named first, and we are named next as a kind of suffix to God's name. Throughout *Mishkan HaNefesh* one finds a balance of creative translations and standard renderings of formulaic phrases. We vary the language in order to assert that no single translation is absolute, and because we have tried not to be dogmatic. One of the worst outcomes of communal worship is boredom; one of its antidotes is diversity of expression, which is thought-provoking, spiritually stimulating, and even disruptive—which is to say, challenging. A new turn of phrase to express a familiar idea (i.e., defamiliarization) can wake us up. And isn't that Maimonides' imperative? "Wake up!" is one of the most-cited themes of the Days of Awe and one of the chief reasons that we sound the shofar.

We now turn to five published translations of one line in the prayer: *V'tein chelkeinu b'Toratecha*. Each translation is different; yet each, in its own way, reflects the purpose of the prayer and its essential idea.

Let Your Torah be our way of life.	*Gates of Repentance* (1978); *Mishkan T'filah* (2007)	Reform
Grant us our share in Your Torah.	*Koren/Sacks* (2006)	Orthodox
Grant us a share in Your Torah.	*Mishkan T'filah* (2007)	Reform
Let the Torah be our portion.	*Maḥzor Lev Shalem* (2010)	Conservative
May each of us find a portion of Torah that is ours.	*Mishkan HaNefesh* (2015)	Reform

The translation in *Mishkan HaNefesh* parallels our translation of *Eloheinu* in the opening line of the prayer: "God who is ours" // "a portion of Torah that is ours." The poetic quality would be only superficial were it not for a deeper meaning in the two phrases. In both cases the words "is ours" in the translation draws attention to a personal relationship: between us and God, between us and Torah. In the phrase "May each of us find . . ." we are not asking God to "grant" or to "let" the Torah be ours; we are asserting our role and responsibility in this process: "May we find it because we are seeking it." The formulation "May we find . . ." infuses the prayer with the dimension of human choice. This emphasis is informed by the ideas of Rabbi David Hartman (1931–2013),[5] who teaches the significance of "human dignity and adequacy" in our relationship with God—a relationship in which human beings exercise freedom and autonomy. "May each of us find a portion of Torah that is ours" means that each person is actively engaged in a lifelong quest for personal connection with Torah; each of us is a participant in the dynamic project of the Jewish people from Sinai to the present.

An emphasis on human adequacy also informs another aspect of this prayer: "Let Your holy Shabbat be our heritage, embraced freely and with love." The traditional prayer says that God gave Shabbat to the Jewish people as an inheritance "with love and favor" (*b'ahavah uvratzon*). The translation in *Mishkan HaNefesh* again underlines the human dimension: our heritage offers us Shabbat, an extraordinary gift to be "embraced freely and with love." This new translation aims to make us attentive to the exercise of human freedom—here, in this instance, by choosing to embrace Shabbat as a sign of the love between God and Israel.

5. David Hartman, *A Living Covenant: The Innovative Spirit in Traditional Judaism* (Woodstock, VT: Jewish Lights, 1997).

Closing Words

Behind the faithful translations of *Mishkan HaNefesh* are questions of faith: How do we translate a prayer book's language of faith into a language for living in the real world? How do we penetrate the differences between Hebrew and English, so as to arrive at a common spiritual core? How do we build a living bridge from ancient worlds to our own? And what are the right words, in the twenty-first century, to say what it means to hope and fear, to love God and doubt God, to bless and be blessed?

"Ultimately," writes Rabbi Abraham Joshua Heschel (1907–1972), "the goal of prayer is not to translate a word but to translate the self; not to render an ancient vocabulary in modern terminology, but to transform our lives into prayers."[6] Prayer is not the mechanical substitution of one vocabulary for another; it aims at something more important and profound: the transformation of the self and, perhaps, by extension, the healing of families, communities, and humanity itself.

The King James translators help us reflect on our questions, too: "Translation it is that openeth the window, to let in the light . . ."—that we may see more clearly who we are, where our journey has taken us, and where we want to go. "Translation it is . . . that breaketh the shell, that we may eat the kernel . . ."—which is to say: strip away the superficial to reach the essence, the truth. "Translation it is . . . that putteth aside the curtain, that we may look into the most holy place . . ."—and find there the Source of wisdom, the Source of our aspirations, the Source of goodness. "Translation it is . . . that removeth the cover of the well, that we may come by the water"—to refresh ourselves with the poetry of prayer, and drink from the well of memory and salvation.

---

6. Abraham Joshua Heschel, *Man's Quest for God* (New York: Charles Scribner's Sons, 1954), p. 17.

Restoring and Reclaiming Tradition:
Creative Retrieval and *Mishkan HaNefesh*

Rabbi Leon A. Morris

With the release of *Mishkan HaNefesh* in the summer of 2015, much has been written on the creativity and the responsiveness to contemporary life reflected within this new machzor. Such observations are most certainly accurate. Yet at the same time, *Mishkan HaNefesh* represents the fullest realization of a new approach to liturgical reform. It is, in short, the most "traditional" prayer book ever published by the American Reform Movement.

Prayer book reform was always a significant and defining feature of Reform Judaism, in both Europe and America. Liturgical reform overwhelmingly was grounded in the notion that our prayers should be consistent with our theology. Reforms of this type were reflected in the deletion of phrases that reference a return to Zion, the resurrection of the dead, and the desire to rebuild the Temple in Jerusalem (and even phrases recalling that we once did offer sacrifices there). As Jakob Petuchowski wrote, "Prayer, it was argued, demands absolute honesty; and the corollary was understood to imply that the prayerbook can contain only such statements as are factually correct, literally true, and historically verifiable."[1]

Such criteria seem out of place in twenty-first-century religious life. It is not only that our attitudes have shifted on some of these specific issues (for example, an embrace of Zionism). More than that, we no longer look to our prayer books for theological consistency. We no longer take a literal approach to understanding the words we recite.

---

1. *Prayerbook Reform in Europe: The Liturgy of European Liberal and Reform Judaism* (World Union for Progressive Judaism, 1968.)

Our Reform forebears had a posture of certainty, both about what God is and what God is not; about what God can do and what God cannot. In contrast, our theological perspective tends to be marked by great uncertainty. We are suspicious of almost all absolute truth claims, including those that emanate from our own denominational camp. For many of us, contemporary Jewish theology is less about what we know with certainty and much more about ways of organizing and conceiving of the world. If medieval and modern Jewish theology were prose, ours is a theology of poetry. So, the expectation that any prayer book—itself an anthology of texts reflecting multiple theological positions—must be in line with our own contemporary theology now seems inappropriate, unachievable, and outdated.

The guiding principle of a twenty-first-century Reform prayer book is the notion of "creative retrieval." I first encountered this term in the *CCAR Journal* (Summer 2004) by Rabbi Herbert Bronstein. He defined it as "the retrieval from our own traditional sources and our own roots, from the design of our own liturgy, of meaningful elements relevant to our own time." In the same article, he also borrowed the term *ressourcement* from the Nouvelle Theologie, a mid-twentieth-century school of Catholic theology.

Ressourcement refers to a return to the sources. In its Catholic context, this referred to a return to the Scriptures and the writings of the church fathers. For us, creative retrieval or ressourcement represents an approach to Reform liturgy that is committed to mining the classic words of our sources to see how they might be used or transformed for our own context. This approach is one of the chief philosophical perspectives driving *Mishkan HaNefesh* and can be seen in decisions that were made from beginning to end.

For the editors, the classic machzor itself was the primary referent and touchstone. The liturgical decisions of previous generations of Reform Jews, as reflected in the *Union Prayer Book* and in *Gates of Repentance*, were noteworthy to us. However, each generation needs its own response to the inherited texts of our tradition. The sacred task of shaping Reform liturgy must never be seen as creating a prayer experience from scratch, any more than it is our task to write a new Torah or a new Talmud. A commitment to the project of creative retrieval meant that we did not see the classic machzor as the "Orthodox" prayer book, but as our own, to draw from, to explain, and to adapt.

Creative retrieval requires of us a shift from a "hermeneutic of suspicion" to a hermeneutic of embrace. We are well aware that the classic prayer book was compiled over many centuries. We know that it reflects the perspectives of its times, many of which we find untenable. Indeed, our perspectives on a host of issues that inform the classic prayer book have changed. Our understanding of gender, our commitment to egalitarianism, our understanding of non-Jews and non-Jewish religious expressions, and the non-exilic nature of Jewish life in the Diaspora are but a few of the ways our lives differ from those who wrote the classic prayers. At the same time, a hermeneutic of embrace urges us to see the classic siddur and machzor as the poetry of the Jewish people. A hermeneutic of embrace begins with a love for the classic liturgy and a firm belief that it can be mined for contemporary meaning and relevance. A hermeneutic of embrace is rooted in the idea that the classic text has a great deal to teach us—and that our primary task is to realize how it might be reframed, explained, or translated in such a way as to allow it to live again in our Reform synagogues.

This approach is further buttressed by the renaissance of Jewish learning that has impacted the entire American Jewish community, including our Reform Movement. The phrase "lifelong learning" has become standard. There is today, inside and outside of Reform synagogues, a strong interest and deep love for primary Jewish texts and the rich and varied conversations that emerge from a meaningful encounter with them. Among these primary Jewish texts are surely the classic siddur and the classic machzor. Widespread positive experiences with text study have resulted in an appreciation even for texts that are difficult and challenging in light of contemporary attitudes. Increasingly, twenty-first-century American Jews value opportunities to confront such texts directly and to play a role in trying to derive relevance and meaning from them. The history of reforming the prayer book embraced an approach that assumed that laity would be put off by such texts, or simply would not know what to do with them. Such passivity regarding the texts was part of a wider context for Reform worship in which worshipers were largely observers in a service that was mostly read to them

by their rabbis. In contrast, today's Reform Jews would privilege interpretation over revision. They want to struggle with, and make meaning
from, the classic words themselves, rather than have it done for them by
others.

Of course, there will be parts of the traditional liturgy that will cause
pain or offend—selections that even the most robust commentary will
not be able to rescue. In these cases, the best choice may indeed be to
remove it from our prayers. But such instances are few and far between,
and liturgical reforms such as these represent a miniscule number of
changes Reform has made to the prayer book over the years.

A hermeneutic of embrace rejects claims that "we Reform Jews don't
say this," or that there is such a thing as an authoritative Reform *nusach*.
Such closed determinism has no place in a twenty-first-century approach
to liberal liturgy. Equally important, a hermeneutic of embrace shifts the
burden of proof away from the classic prayers needing to argue their
worthiness for inclusion, to we who must defend why a prayer was not
included, why we changed the words, or why we chose to translate it
metaphorically. A hermeneutic of embrace argues against apologizing
for wanting to restore the traditional text if it can be done in ways that
allow it to inspire, to teach, and or to elicit creative interpretations.
Mishkan HaNefesh is replete with examples of ressourcement or creative
retrieval.

Many (but not all) of the traditional Torah readings were brought
back to the machzor. Genesis 21, the traditional reading for the first day
of Rosh HaShanah that tells of the birth of Isaac and the banishment of
Hagar and Ishmael, was restored. This selection provides the context
for Genesis 22, which is read the next day. It also allows for a wrestling
with Hagar and Ishmael, looking at them through the lens of "the other,"
and even bringing this story to bear in our desire to make peace between
Jews and Arabs. A similar reclamation of traditional readings can be
seen in bringing back part of Leviticus 16, as well as including the entire
Book of Jonah along with the verses from Micah that follow.

The robust sublinear commentary on almost every page of *Mishkan
HaNefesh*, as well as the many selections of "study texts" on the blue
pages, speaks to the desire to reclaim liturgy that had been excluded
from earlier Reform prayer books, and to help those who are praying by

providing the tools to help them appreciate the multi-vocality of the text, with words that speak to the intellect as well as to the soul.

One example of this is found in the ways that the commentary rescues highly particularistic phrases, such as "You chose us" and "Among all the many peoples, you gave us a pathway to holiness" (RH 53, 194; YK 60, 230, 382). Through the sublinear commentary and facing blue "study text" pages, perspectives as diverse as those of Rabbis Gunther Plaut, Abraham Joshua Heschel, Mordecai Kaplan, and Arthur Hertzberg give greater complexity and nuance to this concept—and invite the reader to reinterpret it in ways that speak to the mission and purpose of our people's existence.

This is the first American Reform prayer book to include all three paragraphs of the *Sh'ma* in each and every service. (In some services, the second paragraph and the beginning of the third are on the left-side page in English only; in other services, all three paragraphs appear in Hebrew, transliteration, and English.) The commentary provides a new lens through which to read the challenging theological claims of the second paragraph, and to entertain the possibility that our actions have consequences—even as the most traditional notions of reward and punishment are not true to our own experience.

In language about our hopes for redemption, the editors reclaimed classic phrases that speak of the Messiah as a descendant of David. While earlier Reform liturgy mostly avoided messianic references and almost always revised references to David as his progenitor, in *Mishkan HaNefesh* we are invited to interpret this as "an emblematic figure who shines through Jewish history as a symbol of messianic hope" (RH 50; YK 224).

The centrality of the Thirteen Attributes of Mercy, the *Sh'losh Esreih Midot*, as the leitmotif of the *s'lichot* prayers of Yom Kippur is another example. In Exodus 34:6–7, God recites these attributes at Moses's request to see God's face in the aftermath of the sin of the Golden Calf as he ascends Mount Sinai a second time, with the second set of Tablets he himself has carved. The recitation signals God's compassion and forgiveness. Therefore the Rabbinic tradition (in a midrash included in *Mishkan HaNefesh*, YK 100) understands our recitation of these attributes as reminding God, as it were, of the ability to forgive us. By reciting them over and over again, we suggest that our sins, as serious as they might be, do not compare in magnitude to the sin of the Golden Calf. We are saying to God that if forgiveness was granted for that cardinal sin, then certainly we are deserving of forgiveness as well. The recitation of the Thirteen Attributes appears in every *S'lichot* service but is most pronounced in *Kol Nidrei* and *N'ilah*, providing bookends in which these *s'lichot* are the central motif (YK 96–111, 311, 640–651).

The distinctive phrase *Atah notein yad l'foshim* ("You hold out Your hand to those who do wrong . . .") was restored to the *N'ilah* service. These noteworthy and evocative words that appear traditionally in the context of the final *Vidui* of *N'ilah* are expanded here in *Mishkan HaNefesh* and developed more fully, with three discrete occurrences (YK 618, 630, 654). Understanding the power of this phrase from the classic machzor, our teacher Dr. Lawrence Hoffman first suggested to us that we consider accentuating it as the overriding theme of *N'ilah*. In doing so, we say: "We have spent the day in prayer and fasting. We have devoted the previous ten days (and in many ways the previous forty) to changing our ways. We have done what we can. We have used all the words at our disposal. Now, we look to God to reach out a hand to us."

T'filah Zakah is a prayer recited by individuals at the beginning of Yom Kippur to shape the intention of the day. It is attributed to Rabbi Abraham Danzig (1748–1820) and appears in many *machzorim* since that time. It reflects upon the five prohibitions of Yom Kippur (eating and drinking, sexual relations, anointing oneself, wearing leather shoes, and bathing). In both adaptations in *Mishkan HaNefesh* (YK 10–13), and particularly in the first rendition (pp. 10–11), we have one of the strongest examples of ressourcement in the entire book. The editors knew that many of our congregants do not currently embrace all of these traditional prohibitions. Despite that, our adaptations of *T'filah Zakah* have mined these as spiritual practices that carry important messages for each and every one of us, irrespective of our level of observance.

Finally, *Seder HaAvodah*, "the *Avodah* service," is a creative construct that draws its basis from both the classic machzor as well as the biblical account of the High Priest on Yom Kippur from Leviticus 16. While only a few discrete parts of this service parallel the traditional *Seder HaAvodah*, the entire service is composed as a way of placing the ancient

rite of Yom Kippur front and center in our consciousness and imagination. The fifteen steps of this service parallel the fifteen steps into the
ancient Temple in Jerusalem. The drama of the High Priest entering
the Holy of Holies, confessing for the sins of Israel, and emerging whole
is the fuel that powers the creative development of this service. The
introduction of the service (YK 446) encourages us to find in the ancient
sacrifices and rites treasured "family heirlooms" that "tell us who we
are, by showing us where we came from." Revisiting the story of Yom
Kippur's original observance addresses our own contemporary spiritual
needs. The ancient rites speak to our own desire to connect to God, and
to understand that our actions can bring us closer or make us more distant from God. The story of *Seder HaAvodah* is about our desire to give
and our longing to begin again.

Utilizing a hermeneutic of embrace raises the bar for the work of
liberal liturgy. It is much easier to delete and to change than to explain,
to "translate" (understood narrowly and broadly), or to use in new ways.
A hermeneutic of embrace with respect to liturgy urges us to expand
our understanding of prayer as *avodah*. Most commonly, we explain that
prayer is *avodah* because it is a form of service, *avodah shebalev* (service
of the heart). However (as I learned from Dr. Elie Holzer from Bar-Ilan
University), the understanding of *avodah* as "work" might be apt as well,
when we consider the interpretive labor required of us when trying our
best to bridge the gap between the inherited words of the classic siddur
and our contemporary lives. It is often hard work to make meaning from
these words. Simultaneously, such work is a privilege, a blessing, and an
opportunity for connection and continuity.

Mishkan HaNefesh represents a noteworthy and significant turn in the
way American Reform Jews approach liturgy. Counter to the approach
of more than a century, among the many things we tried to achieve was
to restore rather than to reform, and to reclaim rather than discard.
Much of its creativity emerges from a desire to embrace. In countless
examples it enables contemporary American Jews to find their voices
among the words of the classic machzor.

*This essay was adapted from "The End of Liturgical Reform as We Know It: Cre-
ative Retrieval as a New Paradigm," CCAR Journal: The Reform Jewish Quarterly (Summer 2013): 29–34.*

What Happens When We Use Poetry in Our Prayer Books—and Why?

Rabbi Sheldon Marder

In memory of Rabbi Scott Corngold (1962–2011)

A Way of Connecting

One of my teachers, West African writer Kofi Awoonor, always began his poetry workshops with an enthusiastic pronouncement like this one: "Poetry is life! I could not live without it." Kofi knew better than to use the word "spirituality" in a college classroom in 1969; but thirty years later Edward Hirsch could give full expression to the true motivation behind Kofi's exuberance:

> Reading poetry is a way of connecting—through the medium of language—more deeply with yourself even as you connect more deeply with another. The poem delivers on our spiritual lives precisely because it simultaneously gives us the gift of intimacy and interiority, privacy and participation. . . . I understand the relationship between the poet, the poem, and the reader not as a static entity but as a dynamic unfolding. An emerging sacramental event. A relation between an I and a You. A relational process.[1]

Hirsch unlocks my teacher's enigmatic pronouncement: poetry is life because it is "a way of connecting. . . . a relational process." And, for a num-ber of reasons, which we will explore in this essay, poetry is uniquely suited to the task of bringing the gifts of connection and "dynamic unfolding" into the Jewish worship experience.

Modern Poetry in Our Prayer Books: A Brief History

Current discussion on the use of poetry in the prayer book is indebted

---

1. Edward Hirsch, *How to Read a Poem* (New York: Harcourt Brace, 1999), 4–5.

to years of public discourse on the subject. In 1981 Rabbi Herbert Bronstein wrote a proposal entitled "Suggested Program for T. Carmi on Prayer Book Enhancement/Revision." T. Carmi (whose major anthology, *The Penguin Book of Hebrew Verse*, appeared in print that year) would be given the task of providing the CCAR with liturgical and nonliturgical Hebrew poetry—evocative texts to encourage "engagement, aspiration, quest, searching, [and] affirmation." T. Carmi's extant files include Hebrew poems related to all of the major rubrics and themes of the Shabbat liturgy, as well as some translations by members of the CCAR. The project was meant to be didactic (informing liberal Jews of our "spiritual treasury"), preservationist (saving the *piyutim* of modern Hebrew writers), and, most of all, liturgically creative (using Hebrew poems in translation to "open up or develop" the siddur's motifs and themes). T. Carmi's contribution would be noted posthumously twenty-six years later on the Acknowledgments page of *Mishkan T'filah* (2007).

Early examples of modern poetry in Reform prayer books can be seen in the CCAR's *A Passover Haggadah* (1974) and in *Gates of Prayer* (1975); in *Gates of Repentance* (1978) Rabbi Chaim Stern placed the poems most prominently in *Avodah*—for example, Jacob Glatshteyn, Avraham Shlonsky, Haim Lensky, Chaim Nachman Bialik—though several poems appear elsewhere (e.g., Rainer Maria Rilke, Anthony Hecht). The Israel Movement for Progressive Judaism's 1982 *Ha'Avodah Shebalev* made significant use of modern poetry (both Hebrew and Yiddish), inspiring a generation of creative liturgists, and laid the groundwork for *Siddur Erev Shabbat* of the Tel Aviv community Beit T'filah Yisraeli (2011).

The Reconstructionist Movement made a strong statement about the value of poetry by choosing a professional poet (Joel Rosenberg) to translate the liturgy for its *Kol Haneshamah* series (1996, 1998, and 1999), which included poems by non-Jewish as well as Jewish writers.

The CCAR's *On the Doorposts of Your House* (1994) also includes non-Jewish works in its nearly forty pages of poems: pillars of English and American literature like Wordsworth, Shelley, Dickinson, and Stevens are side by side with superb Hebrew and Yiddish writers such as Abba Kovner and Kadya Molodowsky. The editorial team for *Doorposts* envisioned Reform Jews enhancing their home rituals and personal spiritual practices with world-class poetry.

By the time Rabbi Elyse Frishman led the CCAR's creation of *Mish-kan T'filah* (*MT*), decades of discourse and experimentation had laid a strong foundation for the pervasiveness of modern *piyutim* in Reform prayer books. With *MT*'s publication in 2007, the poetry of Bialik, Lea Goldberg, and Yehuda Amichai was now fully at home among the works of Solomon ibn Gabirol, Yehuda Halevi, and the Psalmists. Some rabbis expressed the fear that worshipers would prefer the twentieth-century Yehuda to his Spanish namesake.

When the Rabbinical Assembly published *Maḥzor Lev Shalem* in 2010—with an A to Z (Amichai to Zelda) thoroughness, including poets as varied as Admiel Kosman and Denise Levertov—the Conservative Movement completed a trajectory that began with Rabbi Jules Harlow's inclusion of poems by Nelly Sachs, Hillel Zeitlin, and other modernists in his groundbreaking 1972 machzor.

It is clear that all three major liberal movements have advanced the use of modern *piyutim* to reframe and reinvigorate worship along the lines foreseen by the Carmi Project. A box of T. Carmi's files now resides (temporarily) in my office: a symbol, for me, of modern poetry's impor-tance in our spiritual lives. Further, those files encourage us to ask what kind of public dialogue should precede liturgical innovation.

Poetry and Theology

Innovation is one of the core ideas in Jewish prayer—from the concept of *chidush bitfilah* to the religious creativity of the great medieval poets. Why did the *pay'tanim* innovate in the ways they did? How does one explain the impulse to incorporate their poems in the prayer books of our people? Although these questions are beyond the scope of this essay, a few words on this subject by Rabbi Jakob Petuchowski are most useful:

> Theology is compelled to rely on intimations. When we speak
> of something *of* which we only have hints and intimations, we
> can speak of it likewise only *in* hints and intimations. We can
> allude to it, and we can suggest it; but we can hardly formu-
> late it in propositions which will pass muster before the bar of
> logical rigor. We had, therefore, best express it in the images
> and the nuances of poetry.[2]

2. Jakob J. Petuchowski, *Theology and Poetry: Studies in the Medieval Piyyut* (London: Routledge & Kegan Paul, 1978), 3.

Guided by the idea that poetry—the genre of image and nuance—is the literary mode best suited to theology, I will take an essentially literary approach to the question I have posed in the title: "What happens when we use poetry in our prayer books—and why?"

Metaphor: Part I

Let's turn first to metaphor, one of the most compelling reasons why poetry "works" in a prayer book. Jorge Luis Borges provides our first example:

> There is a Persian metaphor which says that the moon is the mirror of time. In that phrase, *mirror of time* is the fragility of the moon and also its eternity. It is the contradiction of the moon, so nearly [translucent], so nearly nothing, but whose measure is eternity. To say *moon* or to say *mirror of time* are two aesthetic events, except that the latter is the work of a second stage, because *mirror of time* is composed of two unities, while *moon* gives us, perhaps more effectively, the word, the concept of the moon. Each word is a poetic work.[3]

Think of the word "moon" as the faithful translation of a Hebrew prayer in our machzor. And think of the beautiful Persian metaphor "mirror of time" as a poem on the opposite page. How does the poetic "mirror of time" function in relation to the original prayer, "moon"? What does it accomplish?

For the sake of argument, imagine that, inexplicably, we have lost all reason to pay attention to the moon—the way Jews sometimes lose their appetite for God, angels, and Messiah. The metaphor "mirror of time" invites us to reconsider the moon and ponder its place in our lives from a fresh, new perspective: its dynamic and visible relationship to time. So, too, evocative poetry, with interesting and surprising metaphors for God, can wake up our theological reflection.

Or consider a metaphor spoken by novelist David Grossman in a newspaper interview in 2010:

> [Grossman's] younger son, Uri, was killed in combat in the final hours of the 2006 Lebanon War. . . . "You have to understand," he

---

3. Jorge Luis Borges, "Poetry," *Seven Nights*, trans. Eliot Weinberger (New York: New Directions, 1984), 78.

said, a photo of Uri—uniformed, eyes laughing behind glasses—
on a shelf to his right, "that when something like this happens to
you, you feel exiled from every part of your life. Nothing is home
again, not even your body."[4]

Grossman's metaphor says that losing a child is an extreme form of *galut*
in which feeling "at home" is no longer possible; for this bereaved father,
the emotional reality of home no longer exists as it did before his son's
death. Could a Jewish writer have chosen a more poignant, transforma-
tional metaphor to describe the death of a son? Metaphor has worked its
mysterious alchemy: since the death of his son Grossman is not the same
anymore; and, having read his words, neither are we.

Metaphor: Part II

Philosopher Ted Cohen presents metaphor as an effective way to cultivate and achieve intimacy.[5] Cohen's insight is remarkable and eye-
opening. Let's use Grossman's metaphor to illustrate Cohen's idea.
Notice, for example, how the metaphor instantly draws us into Grossman's inner life and shows us how it feels to be a grief-stricken father.
Through one word, "exile," we feel close to a man we have met only
through a newspaper interview. How does this happen? Edward Hirsch,
excited by the poetic implications of Cohen's idea, describes it this way:

> Cohen argues . . . that the maker and the appreciator of a met-
> aphor are brought into deeper relationship with one another.
> That's because the speaker issues a concealed invitation through
> metaphor which the listener makes a special effort to accept
> and interpret. Such a "transaction constitutes the acknowledg-
> ment of a community." This notion perfectly describes how the
> poet enlists the reader's intellectual and emotive involvement
> and how the reader actively participates in making meaning in
> poetry. Through this dynamic and creative exchange the poem
> ultimately engages us in something deeper than intellect and
> emotion. And through this ongoing process the reader becomes
> more deeply initiated into the sacred mysteries of poetry.[6]

---

4. Ethan Bronner, *The New York Times*, November 17, 2010.
5. Ted Cohen, "Metaphor and the Cultivation of Intimacy," *Critical Inquiry* 5/1
   (Special Issue on Metaphor, Autumn 1978), 3–12.
6. Hirsch, *How to Read a Poem*, 15.

Nothing proves Ted Cohen's point better than the poetry of Yehuda Amichai. In "My Mother on Her Sickbed," Amichai invites us into his mother's room, where we find ourselves face to face with a dying woman he loves. She has "the lightness and hollowness of a person / Who has already said goodbye at the airport / In the beautiful and quiet area / Between parting and takeoff."[7]

Now consider the following words, which the poet spoke to an interviewer: "The impulse to compare your inner world to the world around you is very natural, and this is how a metaphor is born. . . . The right metaphor is the core of my poem."[8] Following his impulse, Amichai discovers in his mother's illness a connection between the airport's "quiet area" (where the passengers have stepped beyond our reach) and the liminal state of a loved one who is actively dying—in transition and inaccessible to her family. The two things linked in this metaphor resonate like notes in a musical chord; and, in the making of metaphor, Amichai had perfect pitch.

Again, we hear the resonance when the poet likens his tallis to a wedding canopy, a parachute, the cocoon of a butterfly—and, in the end, in Hirsch's words, "engages us in something deeper than intellect and emotion":

> Whoever has put on a tallis will never forget.
> When he comes out of a swimming pool or the sea,
> he wraps himself in a large towel, spreads it out again
> over his head and again snuggles into it close and slow,
> still shivering a little, and he laughs and blesses.[9]

That "something deeper" is the spiritual core of our lives. And I suggest that the poet gives us a spiritual thrill in this poem by means of a complex metaphor in which he invites us to join him not only in the act of wrapping a tallis, but also in the religious experience of immersion (*mikveh*). I think, perhaps, Amichai laughs between the shiver and the blessing because of the dizzying beauty of the image he has wrought.

---

7. Yehuda Amichai, *Yehuda Amichai: A Life of Poetry 1948–1994*, selected and trans. Benjamin and Barbara Harshav (New York: HarperPerennial, 1995), 368.

8. Esther Fuchs, *Encounters with Israeli Authors* (Marblehead, Mass.: Micah Publications, 1982), 88.

9. Yehuda Amichai, *Open Closed Open*, trans. Chana Bloch and Chana Kronfeld (New York: Harcourt, 2000), 44.

Our tradition is rich in beautiful metaphors for God. The use of modern poetry does not trump the value of an arresting phrase like *Atik Yomin* or the High Holy Days' defining metaphor, *Avinu Malkeinu*. Tradition is the heartbeat of our liturgy. At the same time, the metaphors we discover in nonliturgical sources matter a great deal for reasons we have now put forth: metaphor awakens and refreshes perception; it cultivates intimacy by encouraging connection, community, and "a relational process"; it opens the door to a poet's inner world—and therefore can encourage us to open the doors to our inner worlds.

The Barrier and the Bridge

But those doors do not open easily. Religious language—prayer language—can be a barrier. For Diaspora Jews, that includes the additional barrier posed by Hebrew. As we thought about offering the Reform Movement a new machzor that speaks to our many constituencies at once (including those who do not know Hebrew, and especially those who struggle—or worse, have stopped struggling—with belief in God), we realized that we needed to build bridges across the many streams of twenty-first-century liberal Judaism. Poetry can be a bridge.

In making a case for the use of poems in pastoral care, theologian Donald Capps speaks of the affinity between poets and pastors:

> The tendency of poets to be explorative, questioning, and tentative, though not spineless or without conviction and a passion for truth, has a natural fit with the kinds of human experience that have been of greatest concern to pastoral care, and with the ways that pastors, in confronting these situations, have found themselves responding to them.[10]

We learn from Capps that poems are helpful in pastoral settings because they raise more questions than they answer. Poems do not preach or dictate to us—they are not dogmatic; rather, they are suggestive, evocative, and open-ended. A poem can turn a statement of belief into a question for our consideration. Writing about one of Robert Frost's most evocative lines ("And miles to go before I sleep"), Jorge Luis Borges writes:

---

10. Donald Capps, *The Poet's Gift: Toward the Renewal of Pastoral Care* (Louisville: Westminster/John Knox, 1993), 3.

Anything suggested is far more effective than anything laid
down. Perhaps the human mind has a tendency to deny a
statement. . . . But when something is merely said or—better
still—hinted at, there is a kind of hospitality in our imagination. We are ready to accept it.[11]

These qualities, which make poetry useful to the pastoral caregiver, also
make it a bridge between traditional liturgical language and a worshiper
for whom that language is a barrier to prayer because it has the sound
of unyielding, dogmatic truth. Poetry in the prayer book can make our
liturgies more pastoral, more inviting, and more intimate.

Modern Poem as *Piyut*

In her poem "Face" (YK 405), Israeli poet Sivan Har-Shefi shows us
how modern verse can function as modern *piyut*: a bridge between a
challenging biblical/liturgical image and contemporary life. Though a
faithful translation of *Birkat Kohanim* need not (perhaps should not)
include the word "face," we cannot deny that the word *panav* refers
literally to God's face—illumined and lifted up in blessing. Consider what
this poem adds when juxtaposed to the Priestly Benediction (p. 404). In
Donald Capps's terms, this is a poem for a pastoral encounter: "explor-
ative though not without conviction." It is, as well, a poem for our liturgy
because, in the right circumstances, the pastoral texture and ambiance of
a modern poem can give theological language a human face, as it were.

A seeker of God's face, Har-Shefi knows well the Psalmist's cry, "How
long will You hide Your face from me?" (Ps. 13:2). Here she first describes the experience of seeing God's face almost everywhere: in fine
clothing and acts of kindness, in the ordinary "miracles" of daily life, in
her husband's embrace, and in her daughter nursing at her breast. She
gathers these "sightings" together as though creating a composite sketch
of God's multifaceted presence. But then we hear urgent echoes of
Psalm 13 as the poet notes the places where she has felt threats to God,
and perhaps even God's absence: the face of war, the face of a parent no
longer available to her, her own face (that is, vanity and the modern cult
of self-worship). In the end, like the author of Psalm 13, the poet affirms

---

11. Jorge Luis Borges, *This Craft of Verse*, ed. Calin-Andrei Mihailescu (Cambridge,
Mass.: Harvard University Press, 2000), 31.

the truth of her experience: God exists and God's face exists—both the idea of God and, more important, the living reality of God in the world: source of protection, grace, and peace.

What's more, by exploring the word *panecha* in a very personal way, and with disarming simplicity and honesty, Har-Shefi (an Orthodox Israeli) might even make non-Hebrew readers curious about the wording of the original prayer and pry open the Hebrew text to those for whom it would otherwise be a barrier or, at least, a mystery.

The Challenge of a Poem

Is a poem like "Face" too confusing for worshipers? Writes Rabbi Yochanan Muffs:

> Every poem is a challenge to our total being: our senses, our intelligence, and our soul. We are afraid to confront the poem head-on (or at all) because we may be found lacking in the balance. Poems are written in a special language, and even though we instinctively know this, to defend ourselves, we dismiss poems as "only poetry." Thus, most people act in one of two ways: they either reject poems as silly or they read them literally. However, to read them literally is to overlook the fact that every poetic statement is a compromise between what is seen and what can be said in the limit of words.[12]

"Face" may well be a challenging poem for many worshipers. But is it any harder to decode than, say, the familiar words "*ya·eir Adonai panav eilecha vichuneka*"? What does that sentence actually mean? There are a great many ideas in our prayer books that require enormous effort to explain or defend; but often we allow the claims and assertions of our liturgy to wash over us without giving them the thought they deserve.

I suggest that poetry in the prayer book is an invitation to greater mindfulness—thought, reflection, and contemplation. But, most of all, a poem invites us to join the poet in the act of imagining and wondering. For example, what might the image "God's face" mean? What does it suggest to us, as a Jewish idea or on a personal level? "Every poem," says Muffs, "is a challenge to our total being." Instead of fearing that our

---

12. Yochanan Muffs, *The Personhood of God: Biblical Theology, Human Faith, and the Divine Image* (Woodstock, Vt.: Jewish Lights, 2005), 106–107.

interpretation of a poem will be wrong or inadequate, we can learn from poets to be playful and inventive—discovering in metaphor, rhyme, and alliteration ways to expand the territory between what we see and what we are able to say with words. That territory, it seems to me, is the very place where we experience what we call spirituality and God.

A Glimpsed Alternative

I think about the prayer *Asher Yatzar* (YK 156) as I read the lines by May Sarton (p. 157). Their brevity encourages us to slow down and focus closely on each word or phrase: the sweetness of "old friend"; the harshness of "enemy"; the soft, slant rhyme of "help" and "cope"; the modesty of "I shall try"; the poignancy of "to the end." The prayer, too, is a "close reading" of the body, suggesting that we focus and reflect on every wondrous detail of our physicality: the openings, the arteries, the organs.[13]

The prayer *Asher Yatzar* views the human body with wonder, appreciation, and gratitude. The poet sets forth a view of the aging body that is marked by tenderness, compassion, and forgiveness. Each work, in its own way, presents a countercultural perspective that challenges the message we receive from the secular world—that beauty resides only in the youthful and "perfect" body.

The poem, of course, differs from the prayer in a most significant way: the poet addresses her body, not God. And yet Sarton's poem strikes a deeply spiritual chord as she considers the choice that is entirely hers to make—and then makes it with humility and dignity. The prayer attributes the body's grandeur to its Divine Maker. The poem emphasizes, instead, the crucial function of human attitudes and perceptions in determining our view of the body. Thus it honors the idea of human adequacy and initiative that is a counterweight to the traditional theology of Jewish prayer.[14] Both *Asher Yatzar* and the poem offer, in the words of poet Seamus Heaney, "a glimpsed alternative, a revelation of potential that is denied or constantly threatened by circumstances."[15]

---

13. From the translation of the prayer *Asher Yatzar* in *Maḥzor Lev Shalem*, ed. Edward Feld (New York: The Rabbinical Assembly, 2010), 35.

14. See David Hartman, *A Living Covenant: The Innovative Spirit in Traditional Judaism* (Woodstock, Vt.: Jewish Lights, 1997).

15. Seamus Heaney, *The Redress of Poetry* (New York: The Noonday Press—Farrar, Straus and Giroux, 1995), 4.

Sarton's poem puts human flesh on the theological bones of *Asher Yatzar*. In a sense, this is a central task of all poetry in the prayer book: to help us make the language of prayer, which can be abstract, alienating, and remote, into something concrete, inviting, and deeply personal. The Torah promises that God's teaching is "not too baffling for you, nor is it beyond reach. . . . No, the thing is very close to you, in your mouth and in your heart, to observe it" (Deut. 30:11, 14). Poetry can bring the teachings of Jewish tradition close to us. Through compelling, evocative language that is "experience-near," the right poem helps us open our hearts to the ineffable.[16]

What's more, poetry offers us an opportunity for *tikkun* (an act of healing, repair, and perhaps even transformation). May Sarton's words show us a woman, entering her ninth decade of life, who is powerfully resisting the social forces that tell her that old age is an enemy and her body a source of frustration. Here she beautifully exemplifies Wallace Stevens's famous definition of poetry as "a violence from within that protects us from a violence without." Seamus Heaney elaborates: "It is the imagination pressing back against the pressure of reality." It is the power of the imagination, says Heaney, that provides the "redress of poetry"—its ability to heal and make whole, "to place a counter-reality in the scales—a reality which may only be imagined, but which nevertheless has weight."[17]

Writers like Sarton, Amichai, Har-Shefi, and Grossman show us how *tikkun* happens in real life—not suddenly and not perfectly, but as a result of thoughtful reflection, choice, the force of imagination, and will. At its best, poetry celebrates the gift that allows human beings to see things differently, to remake the world and reinterpret received ideas and traditions. This "glimpsed alternative" can be poetry's greatest contribution to our Jewish books of prayer.

This essay was adapted from its original appearance in CCAR Journal: The Reform Jewish Quarterly *(Summer 2013), pp. 16–28.*

---

16. The phrase "experience-near" is from Capps, *The Poet's Gift*, 3.
17. Heaney, *Redress of Poetry*, 1, 3–4, which includes the statement from Wallace Stevens's essay "The Noble Rider and the Sounds of Words."

Integrated Theology:
A New Approach to Understanding the Divine

Rabbi Elaine Zecher

Mishkan HaNefesh uses the approach of Integrated Theology. Integrated Theology juxtaposes and places different, and often contradictory, theological ideas throughout the pages of the machzor. Each concept can stand individually but together, despite the differences, they offer a stronger and more complex understanding of God.

This essay will explore how and why Integrated Theology came about. It will also address the challenge of belief and doubt, and how an Integrated Theology might provide a response to such questions.

For many, the High Holy Day experience and the images and metaphors of the machzor present overwhelming challenges to articulate any concept of God that may resonate. How can a non-believer or a disbeliever enter into such a prayer experience? The wave of High Holy Day images of majesty and sovereignty could drown someone who is already wary and unsure of whom or what God may be.

Mishkan HaNefesh allows each person to enter its pages to discover a pathway toward an understanding of the Divine. Integrated Theology does not espouse one particular way of believing or understanding God. To the contrary, it offers multiple ways to express belief—and even disbelief—and the power of human agency to affect the world. Translations to the prayers yield one understanding, while a counter-text may offer a thoroughly different alternative. One does not need to cancel the other out. Nor is it necessary to choose one over the other.

This is the essence of an Integrated Theology. Like a musical selection with multiple notes interplaying one on top of the other, Integrated Theology allows for dissonant and harmonious ideas to work together, to open up broader possibilities of what it might even mean to express a belief in a greater Power of the universe.

Before we enter *Mishkan HaNefesh*, however, we need to stand at the gates of our past. The story actually starts with *Gates of Prayer*. Those who grew up using this Shabbat and weekday prayer book know that it provided numerous service options. Service One provided the traditional prayers with translations conveying a Sovereign Ruler of the universe. Service Five did not even translate the Hebrew at all, in an attempt to omit God from the English. Other services, through creative translation or a different option altogether, focused on a specific understanding of the Divine. Each service stood alone in its theological presentation.

When it came time to develop a new prayer book, the Editorial team of *Mishkan T'filah*, along with its editor, Rabbi Elyse Frishman, sought to bring more than one voice or idea to the page. The result was the two-page spread with the traditional prayer on the right side and the creative interpretations on the left side. This innovation allowed for more than one perspective of theology to be presented, as well as a broader thematic approach to each prayer.

At first, it might have seemed like an inconsistent presentation to allow dissonant ideas offered together, but it soon became apparent that this methodology allowed a new kind of integrated approach to theology.

Rabbi Frishman wrote, "Theologically, the liturgy needed to include many perceptions of God: The transcendent, the naturalist, the mysterious, the partner, the evolving God. . . . We should sense all these ways. This is the distinction of an Integrated Theology: Not that one looks to each page to find one's particular voice, but that over the course of praying, many voices are heard, and ultimately come together as one."

The idea for an integrated theology comes in part from a medical model. Bridging, contrasting, and learning from different medical modalities such as chemotherapy, acupuncture, surgery, and mindfulness meditation provide an understanding of how bringing together disparate treatments and world views can potentially work toward an enhanced and more person-centric, comprehensive care. In the same way that integrative medicine seeks to engage different therapeutic approaches, both "conventional" and "complementary," to treat an individual, it is possible to apply this idea to the prayer book and machzor. An individual could experience the sacred through a combination of different approaches to God, which then results in a fuller and more holistic understanding of the Divine.

It is important to note, however, that *Mishkan T'filah* did not introduce the multi-voice approach. Honoring and respecting many perspectives is at the heart of Jewish tradition. Any page of the Talmud lays out a vast array of opinions, ideas, and discussion—all in disagreement and concert at the same time. In a similar vein, there is a concept in Judaism called *Eilu va-eilu*: divergent ideas that can contradict and complement at the exact same time receive equal importance and sometimes helps us reach an even better understanding. What is the best way to resolve an argument? You say, "You are both correct." There is an argument in the Talmud, not an uncommon event. Hillel and Shammai are disagreeing. A heavenly voice is heard, also a frequent occurrence in the Talmud, which says *eilu va-eilu divrei Elohim chayim*: "These and also those are the words of the living God." No single answer works all the time. It is a way to include more than one idea at the same time without excluding either one. It is also, arguably, one of the most distinguishing and powerful aspects of Jewish tradition and education. In the Bible, in Rabbinic literature like the Talmud and Midrash, and onward, our tradition is one of pluralism with multiple perspectives and diversity. The intention for *Mishkan HaNefesh* was to bring that same kind of diversity to a deeper, intentional level of discovery on the High Holy Days.

One of the most well-known liturgical pieces for the High Holy Days, *Avinu Malkeinu*, is a good example. The text doesn't need a careful analysis to show that it has the potential to be a self-contained Integrated Theology. Perhaps originally, the use of the terms *Avinu*, our Father, and *Malkeinu*, our King, may have been synonyms to summarize the hierarchical, paternal nature of God. The beauty of liturgy, however, is that it is dynamic; and every translation turns into its own interpretative understanding. *Avinu Malkeinu*, translated as "Almighty and Merciful" as it is in *Mishkan HaNefesh*, transforms the image of God into a range of qualities from Caring to All-Powerful.

The particular presentation of *Avinu Malkeinu* on pages 222–225 in the Rosh HaShanah Morning Service provides a helpful illustration. Not only does the presentation of *Avinu Malkeinu* elaborate on these themes even more, but it adds new ones as well, even surprising us at the end. Notice how the use of "Father" and "Mother" intersperse images of "Power" and "Omnipotent" with those of "Gentle" and "Comforting."

The multiplicity of images rolls from one into the other, but they also bump up against each other. Their dissonance invites us in and opens up new possibilities for understanding. The end, then, acknowledges the struggle to believe whether any of it could be true even as we are drawn in as seekers.

The next page (223) offers the "traditional" Janowski version of *Avinu Malkeinu* and addresses God in the pleading fashion we have grown accustomed to in the liturgy. But then on pages 224–225, another concept of God is introduced: The Divine That Is Present Within and Among Us. (See the sublinear note on p. 224.) Through integrating the ideas together, it is possible for there to be a concept of God that includes not only an Almighty and Merciful God, but also the ability of each human being to hold the power of one's own agency to respond as a sacred act.

This is but one example. Turn to any page of *Mishkan HaNefesh* and ask yourself what you might explore or learn about God, and also what you learn about yourself. As one colleague noted regarding our new machzor, "God isn't as high. Then again, we humans are not as low. Both parties play a more balanced and significant covenantal role."

As each person turns to the pages of this machzor, we hope that its images, ideas, prayers, and poetry will strike many resonant chords—and challenging ones as well. In doing so, the sacred encounter between the individual and the community with the Divine may reach new depths of understanding and wholeness.

Collective Effervescence:
High Holy Day Music and Liturgical Memory

Cantor Evan Kent

In the Summer 2013 issue of the *CCAR Journal: The Reform Jewish Quarterly* our colleague and teacher, Dr. Lawrence Hoffman, elaborates on the differences between High Holy Day services that are "done well" and services that are "done right." In his article, Hoffman explained that you can do it right or you can do it well. "Right" according to Hoffman, is liturgy in which all the readings, chants, and actions are followed precisely—but this "doing it right" is often enacted at the expense of doing it "well." A High Holy Day service done well, according to Hoffman, is one in which "one should highlight the traditional prayers and selective modern material that express the deep themes of the High Holy Day season: human sinfulness and nobility, for example, and the promise of life affirmed and renewed" (p. 58). In the interest of doing it "well" Hoffman suggests that we might even

> drop great gobs of the standard material that we now drone through. We should even do away with the *Amidah* on occasion (editing) while retaining some of its holiday insertions— *Uvchein*, for example, duly enlarged with modern readings that emphasize its ultimate faith in universalism. . . . As things stand, *Uvchein* is swallowed up by the usual *Amidah* verbiage that renders it practically invisible. No one even realizes it is there—let alone the reason why. (pp. 58–59)

What Hoffman suggests seems almost heretical to those of us who have spent our lives devoted to making sure that liturgy, *nusach, chazzanut,* and trope are correct. But it actually is not. Hoffman's recommendation follows in the great tradition of liturgical reform where we edit for the sake of brevity and theological and philosophical considerations, and then we highlight to maximize the message of the prayers.

An Expansion of Doing It Well

When worshipers leave a prayer service, they walk through the door with the instantaneous feelings and immediate memories received from the presented liturgy. The songs, sermon, encounters with friends, and mingling with other congregants resonate and resound in their minds. In the subsequent weeks, months, and years, worshipers create an individual and communal memory of the event. When the liturgy is especially potent, these memories are particularly vibrant, and are recalled with great fondness and vitality. Expanding upon Hoffman's original concept of "doing it well," I propose that this "doing it well" implies the creation of deep-seated and long-lasting memories that are not just internalized mentally, but actually become physically embodied and incorporate all the senses.

Sociologists, social psychologists, and anthropologists such as Emile Durkheim, Maurice Halbwachs, Yosef Yerushalmi, Pierre Nora, and Paul Connerton have understood how lively and transformative rituals succeed in creating deeply implanted memories for both the individual and the collective. When we "do it well," we create ritual that has long-lasting impact and becomes implanted in our memories. Music becomes central to "doing it well," as so much of the text we employ in Jewish ritual is either sung or chanted.

The High Holy Day liturgy, in general, and specifically our new machzor, *Mishkan HaNefesh*, provide significant challenges for doing it "well." The High Holy Day liturgy is rich and complex, and especially in *Mishkan HaNefesh*, clergy teams might want to share all the nuances and treasures of the new machzor with the congregation—but this is infeasible and impractical, as services would be unwieldy in length, and it is plausible that the liturgical message of the holidays would be muted by the duration of the services.

How can we do it "well," where "well" implies creating living liturgical memories involving the body and mind? Music, of course, here is key, and in this next section, I provide a few methods that music can aid in the building of liturgical memory.

Use Nusach to Build Memory

In "How Societies Remember," Paul Connerton acknowledged that effective rituals are repetitive, and this repetition implies a real or imagined connection to the past.[1] When our congregants hear *nusach*—the specific liturgical melodies reserved for particular moments and times within the liturgical calendar—they are connected through these musical motifs to previous generations. The melody of the High Holy Day *Bar'chu*, for example, provides worshipers with a melodic cue informing them that the time for Rosh HaShanah and Yom Kippur has arrived, and it permeates much of what is sung on the High Holy Days. Since this musical motif is so memorable and so powerful, we might find other opportunities for including this short melody as a part of the liturgy.

This basic motif of High Holy Day *nusach* could be employed in the section of morning blessings: *Nisim Sheb'chol Yom* (RH 124–128). Although a traditional chant is routinely used, the utilization of this *nusach* would further reinforce the High Holy Day *nusach* and add another moment in the liturgy where the congregation could unite together in song.

Similarly, this readily accessible melody could be used in the Yom Kippur *Avodah* service in *Mishkan HaNefesh*, and in turn, would again, through a congregational melody, assist in bringing the worshipers closer together. In the *Avodah* service, each of the fifteen steps (or *aliyot*) of this service concludes with a *chatimah*, a final blessing. Using the *Bar'chu* melody as the music for the *chatimah* permits the entire congregation to join in song and coalesce as a community.

Opening Songs and Closing Songs

Thomas Turino, in his book *Music as Social Life*, noted how music that is participatory and with an *open form*—that is, not with a predetermined beginning and ending—is often the most effective for creating community and social bonding. Turino explained that *open form* "refers to music that is open ended and can be repeated for as long as the participants and situation requires" with the entire form being repeated over and over.[2]

---

1. Paul Connerton, *How Societies Remember* (Cambridge: Cambridge University Press, 1989).
2. Thomas Turino, *Music as Social Life: The Politics of Participation* (Chicago: The University of Chicago Press: 2008), 37.

In our tradition, the corpus of *niggunim* fall into this category. *Niggunim*, as we know, provide an opportunity for maximum participation by creating a musical environment where the initial melody is easy to learn, and the words or syllables sung are readily accessible. As the *niggun* progresses, participants often create harmony, counter melodies, and add a rhythmic background with claps and foot stomps. The use of *niggunim* is one way to begin the process of creating community during the High Holy Days, when large gatherings of people who may not know each other take the place of congregants.

Mishkan HaNefesh provides many suggestions for opening songs—songs that I often refer to as "*niggunim* with words." These are short, simple melodies with easily learned lyrics that permit harmonization and improvisation among the congregation. The new machzor includes, for example, "Return Again" by Rabbi Carlebach (RH 6) as one option for commencing the Rosh HaShanah Evening Service. This song fits Turino's criteria for enabling participation. The easy words, combined with the relatively simple melody and the counter melody of the familiar "*Hashiveinu*," provides worshipers with the satisfaction that they are part of a participatory music-making and praying community. The continued repetition, seemingly without end, provides those singing with an overall feeling of well-being, what Turino refers to as "security in constancy."[3] When voices join in song, with melody and harmony, combined with a text that reinforces and amplifies the message of the greater liturgy, a memorable moment is created, and the congregation knows that they are "doing it right." Songs that repeat and seemingly have an improvised form enhance ritual and prayer, and aid in the development of both individual and communal memory. Selections like Carlebach's "Return Again" or "*Havah Nashirah*" (both the "folk" version and the contemporary one by Josh Nelson) are songs that on first glance might be considered simplistic, but their value as musical selections for commencing and concluding our High Holy Day worship should not be underestimated.

Opportunities for Synchronicity and Rhythm

In "Beyond Culture," Edward Hall discusses how in social settings we

---

3. Turino, *Music as Social Life*, p. 40.

begin to move "in sync" with each other.[4] He documents how in public places—airports, city streets, markets—people move in an appropriate rhythm and pace for the specific venue. If this interlocking movement occurs in everyday settings, then the interconnecting of body, rhythm, and community becomes even more apparent in a liturgical setting where rhythm is often the guiding force of the ritual.

When highly repetitive forms of music are presented in a ritual setting, they do not lead to boredom, as some might suspect. Rather, repetitive music with a strong rhythmic pulse leads to the "collective effervescence" that Durkheim researched.[5] In this state of effervescence, a community comes together and individuals feel unified, momentarily losing themselves in the worship experience. When we come together to pray on Rosh HaShanah and Yom Kippur, we comprise a collective yearning to hear and experience the messages of these Days of Awe. Highly repetitive music actually adds to the intensity of the ritual—as it enables maximum participation. This feeling of communal synchrony is further enhanced when we add the element of rhythm. When we all feel the life-pulse of music in our liturgies, we feel we belong to the greater ritual society.

A skillful and sensitive percussionist can enhance almost any musical piece in any setting. Although we generally associate the use of percussion in our services with the faster dance-like tunes used, for example, in Torah processions, the subtle beat of drums and other percussion instruments can enhance High Holy Day liturgical selections and provide the synchrony that Hall speaks about. Using percussion during such classic pieces like Max Janowski's *Avinu Malkeinu* might seem heretical to some, but from personal experience, I can attest that subtle percussion enhances the heart-beat nature of Janowski's accompaniment. Even chant-like melodies benefit from the addition of artistically added percussion. Josh Nelson's setting of *Avinu Malkeinu* (*Shirei Mishkan HaNefesh*, p. 55) is a brilliantly written new setting of these ancient words. The rising melody line would be beautifully enhanced with the addition of subtle drumming.

---

4. Edward Hall, *Beyond Culture* (Garden City, N.Y.: Anchor, 1977).
5. Emil Durkheim, *The Elementary Forms of Religious Life*, transl. C. Cosman (New York: Oxford University Press, 2001).

Even High Holy Day chant can be enhanced with the creative application of percussion. For example, re-imagine the *nusach* setting of the confession *Al Cheit* in *Shirei Teshuvah* (2000, p. 280) with the accompaniment of percussion and a metrical vocal line. With the strong steady pulse of both the vocalist and the percussion, this confessional has an incredibly earnest feeling that would be felt by the congregation.

"Doing It Well"

There is no one recipe or floor-plan for "doing it well"; everything that I suggest here is a potential way of enhancing that path, through music, to discovering this concept of "wellness" for each congregation. "Well" entails the creation of profound and deep positive liturgical memory that is embedded in the body and mind. Doing it "well" requires that we need to take risks with our liturgy and our music: to edit, to highlight, and to keep reminding ourselves what are the essential messages of these *Yamim Noraim* and how we can create a liturgical message that resonates and is recalled—not just for a few minutes, but for a lifetime—within the hearts, souls, and minds of our congregants.

How Do We Read This?
The Artwork in *Mishkan Hanefesh*

Rabbi Hara E. Person

Rabbi Judah taught in the name of the Rav: "Any [Torah]
letter that is not surrounded on all four sides by a margin
of [white] parchment is invalid."
—Talmud M'nachot 29a

The editors of *Mishkan HaNefesh* made a bold choice to include abstract art in the new machzor. These eleven wood block prints, placed at the beginning of each volume as a frontispiece and at the start of each service, provide a visual encounter in the midst of a primarily textual and aural experience. Our tradition teaches that the Torah was initially a combination of "black fire" and "white fire." The Talmud discusses the importance of the white space around the black letters, considering the white to be another—albeit hidden—kind of Torah text (*M'nachot* 29a). Both texts are critical to the whole, even as they elicit different ways of reading. As Rav Kook taught, "The Sages explained that these separations allowed Moses to reflect upon and absorb the previous lesson. In other words, the white fire corresponds to the loftier realm of thought and contemplation" (in *Gold from the Land of Israel*). The art in *Mishkan HaNefesh* is like the white space around the written text: it is an invitation to experience the metaphors and imagery of the High Holy Days using a different kind of language, a different kind of metaphor, perhaps even a different part of our soul.

One of the things I remember most distinctly from a college English seminar was the question: "How do we read this?" Most often, it was applied to a text—a poem, a passage in a novel, or an essay. At times, however, the question was directed to a visual image. We would study a piece of art or a photo from a newspaper and "read" it. My professor taught us to be readers of signs, symbols, and visual imagery, pushing us to analyze the world around us in the same way that we engaged with the written word. His goal was to enable us to become nimble critical thinkers, able to explore, probe, and question anything we confronted.

When reading a text we, by necessity, bring ourselves to that text. Our reading is a meeting of our own unique set of experiences and references, and those of the author's. Midrash *Exodus Rabbah* 5.9 teaches that the manna which sustained the Israelites while they wandered in the desert tasted different for each person. Just as each person tasted the manna in a different way, so too does each of us process and understand a text uniquely. Indeed, each time we read a text, we read it differently based on who we are in that moment.

So it is with reading art. More relevant than what the artist meant to convey is what we see. Each of us will have our own understanding of an image. All the various elements in a piece of art become part of the language of that art-as-text. The colors, the white space, the border (or lack thereof), the texture, the particularities of the wood grain, the density of the ink, the shapes—all of these form the language of each piece of art. And just as with any written text, there is no single right interpretation.

Art is a language. Each image creates a new world, a singular and uninhibited space for experience and interaction. Abstract art, like the art of Joel Shapiro that appears in *Mishkan HaNefesh*, may at first glance seem hard to read, as impenetrable as an unfamiliar foreign language. Yet the question we must ask is not "What does it mean?" but rather "What *can* it mean?"

One of the goals of the editorial team in creating *Mishkan HaNefesh* was to allow for diverse doorways into the High Holy Day experience. We sought to provide different modalities of experience through the use of varied types of content. For some, the beautiful translations of the liturgy speak to them as they make their way through the High Holy Days. Others find a way into meaning through the poetry that is interwoven with the liturgy and translation in the book. There are those for whom the music is going to be what makes their experience meaningful, or perhaps it will be the rabbi's sermon. The material meant for personal reflection and meditation, or the intellectual or philosophical commentaries on the bottom of each page might be what presents an avenue into sacred time, space, and thought for yet other participants.

The editors spoke at length about adding visual art as one more doorway in for the visually inclined worshiper. We considered many different ideas before concluding that abstract art would be the best fit for the machzor. We also decided to use art entirely from one artist's body of work. Once we narrowed down our criteria, the question of art was still complex. We wanted art that would enhance the beauty of the text and be a fitting companion to it, art that would speak to the big themes of High Holy Day liturgy. We were also confronted by the parameters set by printing and reproduction.

In our search, we were introduced to the artist Joel Shapiro. Shapiro is an internationally acclaimed artist with pieces in major museums and other settings throughout the world. When we showed him some of the initial drafts of *Mishkan HaNefesh*, he was immediately intrigued by the challenge. During an afternoon spent in his huge, airy, art-filled studio, we were equally intrigued by him and by his work. A short while later, he told us that he was inspired and moved by *Mishkan HaNefesh*, and he offered to create a series of original prints for us.

After thinking about different ways to create the pieces, Shapiro proposed working with wood block prints. These prints would reproduce well on the printing press being used for the book. Practicalities aside, we loved the idea of using wood to create the art for the machzor. The associations were rich and plentiful; the Torah as a tree of life (*eitz chayim*) came to mind immediately. We also were moved by the association with the earth and nature, and the insertion of the natural world into a body of analytical, intellectual, and spiritual ideas.

Shapiro spent months reading the drafts of *Mishkan HaNefesh* and studying High Holy Day liturgy. He worked first with paper: drawing, cutting, and tearing shapes as he pondered the best way to represent the major ideas of the High Holy Days. To prepare for his work, the editors offered him a list with a theme for each service. The comments that follow below are subjective interpretations of the art, gleaned from conversations with the artist. These ideas are meant to be helpful ways to get started when viewing the art. However, they are not intended to limit interpretation. They are not what the art is definitively "about"—they represent only some of the possible readings.

As you consider these pieces keep in mind the following: Reading art is like reading poetry, using visual language rather than verbal. Look at the image. What does it evoke? Rather than trying to understand what it means, try to experience it. Does it feel full or empty? Does it give you a sense of hope, sadness, communality, or a sense of being alone? Does it make you think about fear, courage, or buoyancy? Does it reach out joyfully into the future, or does it feel tentative or grasping? Is it turned back on itself, or does it seem open and inviting? Does it feel uncomfortably raw, breathtakingly beautiful, or both? Is it sure of itself or perplexing? Once you have a sense of your own experience, your reading, of the art, you can ask, "How can these images be visual translations for the over-arching themes of the High Holy Days? How do these images convey awe? *T'shuvah*? *Cheshbon hanefesh*? Forgiveness?"

RH ii: *Frontispiece for Rosh HaShanah.* There is a sense of this piece as being a portal or doorway into the High Holy Days. The section on the left that is folded back creates an opening, which also conveys the idea of parts coming together to make a whole—a fitting idea for the ingathering of the community on the eve of Rosh HaShanah.

RH xxxi: **Rosh HaShanah Evening:** *Avinu Malkeinu, renew us.* This piece conveys a feeling of gathering, ingathering, and homecoming, like the sense of a synagogue as a true *beit k'neset*, a house of gathering together.

RH 101: **Rosh HaShanah Morning:** *Hear the call of the shofar!* The shape at the center is a biologically accurate rendering of a heart. Combined with the circularity of the image, this piece is an intriguing choice for the service that contains the sounding of the shofar. The spiraling provides a feeling of sound and emotionality that connects to the experience of hearing the shofar, the heart of this service.

YK ii: ***Frontispiece for Yom Kippur.*** In this image there is a feeling of being broken and off-kilter. The shapes emphasize the uniqueness of the day and the idea that we are meant to be outside of our usual comfort zones on Yom Kippur. There's also a hint here of the concept that the purpose of Yom Kippur is to explore our internalities, represented here by the texture of the wood-grain inside the shapes.

YK xxxiii: **Yom Kippur Evening: *I forgive, as you have asked.*** The slight bend in the image feels like an apt metaphor for asking forgiveness, conveying a subtle sense of brokenness within the whole. The very simplicity of this piece also provides a fitting beginning to Yom Kippur, when we're stripped down to our core, looking for light in the darkness.

YK 129: **Yom Kippur Morning: *You stand this day, all of you, in the presence of Adonai your God.*** This image embodies a sense of community, a oneness de-spite all the different shapes and types. In this piece we experience a tension between our internal and external selves.

YK 321: **Yom Kippur Afternoon: *You shall be holy.*** Parts of a whole are being brought together in this piece. Each block is individual and unique, but together they form an overlapping, interconnected community.

YK 441: ***Seder HaAvodah: May we ascend toward the holy.*** This is an abstract interpretation of the steps leading up to the Temple—the ascension toward holiness. There is also an unfolding of layers that take us back to the core of the Holy of Holies, and thus also to the core of ourselves, imbued with tension between holiness and the profane.

YK 513: *Eileh Ezk'rah: For these things I weep…*
This is a difficult, agonized image that evokes a
tormented tear, a body twisted in pain, and a display
of deep mourning. The raw, ragged edges that frame
this piece and disrupt the neat orderliness of the
page mirror the way that our history as Jews is punctuated by episodes of tragedy.

YK 535: *Yizkor: These are the lights that guide us
… These are the ways we remember.* This image is
strong and mournful, yet also embodies a sense of
peace and unification. Even as it speaks of emptiness,
we see here the circularity and fullness of the life
cycle. The wood grain reaches upward and forward
into the future and hopefulness, even as it absorbs
and carries with it a sense of loss. The jagged edges
of the print echo the messiness of living, in which
there are no neat boundaries.

YK 609: *N'ilah: You hold out Your hand.* This image
represents the end of the cycle and the path forward.
We see here the way in which *N'ilah* brings us to a
focus on ascension, a path to holiness, and then the
closing of the gates, the light at the end of a tunnel.
We move back toward God as the gates begin to close.

Art doesn't have to be understood in order to be felt. These pieces
can evoke emotion that goes beyond words. They offer a non-verbal way
to connect with some of the central High Holy Day tropes, with the
acts of reflection and repenting, remembering and hoping, celebrating
and grieving, questioning and confessing, forgiving and asking for
forgiveness.

Let yourself experience the art in *Mishkan HaNefesh*. Move beyond
the discomfort of not knowing what to do with it, and just look at it.
Our prayer book is full of metaphors and imagery that don't necessarily

make rational sense. Nonetheless, they move us and connect us with the Divine, and with the big questions of life and eternity. Art is a form of graphic poetry, a language of visual metaphors that gives us another way to engage with the rich, complex experience of the High Holy Days.

Part 3
Indexes and Tables

N.B. As the primary authors of *Mishkan HaNefesh*, Rabbi Janet Marder and Rabbi Sheldon Marder composed the following: all prayers, commentaries, readings, and poems that are not otherwise attributed; the faithful translations of the Hebrew prayers and the Torah and haftarah portions; the translations and interpretations of passages from Tanach, Talmud, Mishnah, Midrash, and other traditional sources, as well as the translation of modern Hebrew poems and medieval *piyutim* that are not otherwise attributed; the adaptations of "legacy prayers" (from sources such as the *Union Prayer Book*, *Gates of Prayer*, and *Olat Tamid*); and the introductory comments on liturgical rubrics, services, and individual prayers. In addition, they conceptualized and wrote a series of original liturgies for Yom Kippur afternoon—*Minchah*, *Avodah*, *Eileh Ezk'rah*, and *Yizkor*.

We thank them—as well as the many authors, poets, scholars, liturgists, and songwriters whose contributions appear in the following indexes.

Index of Themes

RH = Rosh HaShanah volume; YK = Yom Kippur volume; *s* = sublinear commentary.

(Asked the Chofetz Chayim), 377 (Rava asked), 383 (Even if one has a genuine grievance), 387 (God called to Israel), 393 (As the navel is in the center), 399 (Our Sages teach), 407 (*Sim Shalom*: The Blessing of Peace; Our Sages teach; Sang the psalmist), 409 (Upon giving birth), 411 (Acceptable to You), 413 (I do not want to beg forgiveness), 450 (Fifteen Songs of Ascent in the Book of Psalms), 461 (At the time of Creation), 466 (When human beings build a house), 469 (Our Sages teach), 484 (But our Sages taught; Asked Rashi), 486 (Our Sages teach), 487 (Rabbi Meir said), 488 (Rain exists forever), 497 (Asks the Midrash), 505 (What does this verse imply?; Whoever performs), 506 (Once, as Rabbi Yochanan), 507 (Rabbi Yochanan and Resh Lakish taught), 520 (When the time came to say the morning *Sh'ma*), 559 (They said in the name of Rabbi Meir), 590 (There are ten strong things), 623 (It is written; Taught Dov Baer; One of the Sages taught), 627 (When greeting a friend), 641 (When you are asked).

Non-Jews in the congregation:
RH 231 (Torah blessings suitable for non-Jews), 231*s*, 270 (Prayer for the Congregation); YK 259 (Torah blessings suitable for non-Jews), 259*s*, 284 (Prayer for the Congregation).

Questions for personal reflection and/ or discussion: RH 221; YK 308–9; *Minchah Amidah* 359, 362, 367, 381, 397, 403; *Yizkor* 554, 560, 566, 578, 584, 591, 596.

"Recognizing the good" and self-for-giveness: YK 93 (For Acts of Healing and Repair), 312 (*Hakarat HaTov*), 313 (For Every Act of Goodness), 385 (Rabbi Shimon taught; Forgiving Yourself) 424 (For Acts of Healing and Repair), 425 (*Hakarat HaTov*), 581 (Forgive-ness and the Afterlife), 659 (*Hakarat HaTov*), 667 (Love after Love).

Resurrection and the afterlife:
RH 47*s* (In life and in death), 181 (I speak these words but I don't believe them; a counter-text for *Untaneh Tokef*); YK 543 (Where Does It End?), 560 (I sat down), 577 (What Happens after Death?), 581 (Forgiveness and the Afterlife), 582 (Bright Mariner), 586 (If life is a pilgrimage), 603 (If every life were like a drop of rain), 627*s* (*G'vurot*).

Reward and punishment and environ-mental consciousness: RH 14 (The poem of creation), 29*s* (If, indeed you obey), 39 (The Pond in Winter), 63 (In the Name of the daybreak), 155 (Med-itation on the *Sh'ma*), 197 (Keeping Quiet), 217 (The medieval notion), 287 (Our calling is to praise—a re-interpre-tation of *Aleinu*); YK 37 (Lest we serve other gods), 37*s*, 43 (The Peace of Wild Things), 69 (A butterfly comes), 75 (It doesn't have to be; Is it not by his high superfluousness); 117 (Our calling is to praise—a re-interpretation of *Aleinu*), 190 (If, indeed, you obey), 190*s*, 307 (*Vidui* for the Twenty-First Century), 373 (The Gift of Awe), 493–96 (Finding Holiness in Nature).

Science and scientists: RH 4–5 (scientif-ic account of creation), 5 (Carl Sagan), 51*s* (Jonas Salk), 105 (Niels Bohr; Jerome Bruner), 127 (Lewis Thomas); YK 181 (Rachel Carson), 223 (Richard Feynman; Albert Einstein), 373 (Albert Einstein), 399 (Ursula Goodenough), 400*s* (Albert Einstein), 457 (reflections on the Big Bang), 493 (Ursula Good-enough).

Scientific language in poetry: RH 171 (Alicia Ostriker's "molecular" cele-bration of the wonders of nature), 213 (Marilyn Nelson's meditation on the submicroscopic particles in dust); YK 495 (Jacqueline Osherow's inscription of sacred DNA in "God's Acrostic"), 500 (Yehuda Amichai's salute to "a man of the exact sciences").

Sexuality and sexual immorality, including adultery: RH 33 (To untie the knots of betrayal); YK 10–11 (Three Meditations), 13 (You created my body with sexuality—part of the *T'filah Zakah*), 88 (Through sexual immorality—part of *Al Cheit*), 91 (Failures of Love), 293 (Because), 297 (A repentant sinner), 308–9 (*Cheshbon HaNefesh*).

Study texts: RH xvi–xxix (Introductory essays); 2–5, 16 ("personal *Hin'ni*" for silent reflection), 31, 48, 81, 93, 104–5, 107, 113–19, 167, 172–73, 183, 199, 236–37, 242, 248–49, 254, 262, 278, 295; YK xvi–xxx (Introductory essays); 3–8, 17, 47, 52, 85, 94, 136–37, 144–55, 163, 205–7, 211, 217, 231, 264–65, 276, 297, 331, 334–36, 341, 343; *Minchah* 354–55, 358–59, 362–63, 366–67, 380–81, 392–93, 396–97, 402–3, 415; 445–56, 616–17, as well as nearly every page of the *Avodah* and *Eileh Ezk'rah* services.

***T'shuvah* and forgiveness**: RH 33 (To break the bonds of anger); YK 49 (From *T'filah* to *Vidui* to *S'lichot*), 83 (When I was young), 85 (Resh Lakish said), 91 (We abuse), 94 (The Essence of Atonement), 109 (The Bronx, 1942), 154–55 (Study: Modern Era), 293 (Because I was angry), 295 (Pride), 297 (For Study and Reflection), 299 (For the sin we committed), 301 (A Personal Confession), 303 (On New Year's Day), 305 (We focused inward; Seven Social Sins), 307 (*Vidui* for the Twenty-First Century), 308 (*Cheshbon HaNefesh*: Introspection and Silent Confession), 314 (Open your heart), 618–19 (In Praise of God's Hands; In Praise of Hands), 635 (*Teshuvah*), 637 (Psalm), 653s (Confes-

sion), 655s (You hold out Your hand).

Theological doubt and struggle, or outright unbelief: RH 43 (Israel, prepare to meet your God!), 65 (Faith), 69 (I Was Never Able to Pray), 75 (*Avinu Malkeinu*: A Prayer for Renewal), 93 (Introduction to Closing Songs), 139 (My lord is not a shepherd), 161 (The beginning of Your word is truth), 181 (I speak these words—a dialogue), 187 (Prayer), 295 (About the Closing Songs); YK 63 (Like smoke above the altar), 73 (Every day I want to speak with you), 113 (*Avinu Malkeinu*: A Prayer of Protest), 177 (Hey, Clockmaker), 199 (I still don't know whom), 235 (It is not easy to forgive God), 238s Receive their prayer), 239 (I Called God), 251 (Hope), 317 (The Mystery of the Necessity to Inform You), 342s (To speak the truth), 436 (It is Written), 464 (My Tithe), 472 (A New Confession—Ours), 621 (Yearning), 645 (So many words), 651 (You are our Beacon), 657 (You Sit, Waiting).

Theology of human empowerment: RH 14s (to do God's work on earth), 25 (God's hands are our hands), 57 (This is the season of God), 121 (Said Rabbi Levi Yitzchak), 125 (We praise You, Adonai), 139 (Beloved Friend—a counter-text for *HaMelech*), 163 (The voice that redeems us comes from within—a counter-text for *MiMitzrayim g'altanu*), 175s (Prayer is not something we do to God), 177 (Just as the shadow), 200 (*Malchuyot*: Accepting Your Sovereignty), 203 (God's Power… and Ours), 203s, 264–65 (The Divine Awakens within us—a counter-text for *Zichronot*), 283 (I know); YK 19 (Give us the strength to keep our promises—a counter-text for *Kol Nidrei*), 160–62 (You are the Source of blessings), 41 (For every exile), 109 (When men were children), 113 (*Avinu Malkeinu*: A Prayer of Protest), 195 (You took us out of the darkness), 197 (Who is like You / among the silent?—a counter-text for *Mi Chamocha*), 213 (The power of this day—a counter-text for *Untaneh Tokef*), 221 (Letter to a Humanist), 244 (May you receive the light), 311 (If I could see God's face), 361 (Kindness of Heart and Hand), 365 (Your power is with us always), 389 (My God), 401 (Holy One, the mystics had names for You), 434 (The Task That Awaits Us), 475 (The Nearness of God), 506 (When evil darkens our world), 509 (In each human hand), 630s (You hold out Your hand), 663 (Soul-Sustainer).

Theology of non-dualism and mystical consciousness: RH 25 (There is nothing but God), 47 (You are . . . the life force surging within all things), 49 (Perceiving all nature as a prayer come alive), 57 (The rule of Unity), 127 (Why! Who Makes Much of a Miracle?), 224–25 (The Divine That Is Present Within and Among Us—a reframing of *Avinu Malkeinu*), 224–25s; YK 177 (What

Color is Grass?), 181 (Like an unbroken current), 185 (*Adonai Echad*: We Proclaim You One), 243 (Tiny Joys), 454–55 (The mystics of the Kabbalah teach. . . . You! You! You!), 490 (Our prayers take aim), 496 (The Delicate Light of My Peace), 603 (If every life).

Unemployment: YK 113 (*Avinu Malkeinu*: A Prayer of Protest), 263 (A Blessing for *Menschlichkeit*).

Universalism: RH xxviii–xxix, 51 (Good people everywhere will celebrate), 70s (all who dwell on earth), 73 (Peace for every race and nation), 84s (And so, Adonai . . . we look to you), 90s (all who dwell on earth), 293s (all who dwell on earth); YK 81s (all who dwell on earth), 118s (Those who do evil), 222s (In your holiness), 372s (We yearn for connection), 675 (*Havdalah* blessing of separation).

Violence and abuse: RH 232 (Preparing for *Birkat HaGomeil*), 232s; YK 260, 260s, 574–75 (For One Who Died by Violence; In Memory of a Parent Who Was Hurtful).

Index of Biblical Citations

RH = Rosh HaShanah volume; YK = Yom Kippur volume

Isaiah, continued

43:10	YK 466
43:12	RH 177
43:25	YK 66, 234, 388
44:2	YK 70
44:22	YK 66, 234, 388
48:4	YK 302
49:2	YK 649
49:3	YK 105
51:13	RH 82, 202; YK 432
52:1	RH 203
54:10	RH 266
54:13	YK 431
55	RH 336
55:1	YK 183
55:6	RH 336
55:6–7	YK 656
55:6–13	RH 338–39
55:7	YK 152
55:12	YK 312
56:7	YK 227, 444, 475
57:15	YK 292
57:19	YK 97
58	YK 264, 275–76
58:1	RH 268, 280
58:1–14	YK 277–78
58:7	YK 136
59:21	RH 266
60:20	YK 548
64:7	YK 102

Jeremiah

1:5	RH 249
2:2	RH 264
3:14	YK 642
3:21	YK 642
11:16	RH 189
17:9	YK 649
18:3–6	YK 102
25:10	YK 247
31:2–20	RH 255–57
31:11	RH 34; YK 40
31:19	RH 257
31:20	RH 254, 264, 265
32:18	YK 7
51:5	YK 633

Ezekiel

2:6	YK 642
3:12	RH 184, 311; YK 218, 368
5:5	YK 393
11:16	YK 483
16:60	RH 264
18:23	RH 180
33:11	YK 658

Hosea

2:17	YK 667
2:21	RH 266
6:6	YK 506
14:2	YK 63
14:2–3	YK 292
14:3	YK 445, 473, 645

Joel

2:13	YK 147
2:15	RH 280

Amos

3:2	RH 53
3:6	RH 279
4:12	RH 43
5:2	YK 168
5:24	RH 193; YK 478
9:7	RH 53; YK 61

Jonah

1–4	YK 344–49
2:4	YK 350
2:5	YK 426
3:10	YK 147

Micah

4	YK 56
4:4	YK 431
6:6–8	YK 505
6:8	YK 61, 436
7:18–20	YK 350

Habakkuk

2:14	YK 431

Zephaniah

1:15–16	RH 2
14:9	RH 203

Zechariah

8:19	YK 403
9:14	RH 280
12:1	RH 82, 202; YK 432

Psalms, continued

65:2	RH 43
66:1–3	YK 459
68:29	YK 649
69:14	RH 110; YK 138
71:9	YK 98, 294, 316
72:19	RH 151
73:22–23	YK 655
73:26	RH 166, 308; YK 645
77	YK 561
81:4–5	RH 15, 280
84:5	RH 132, 304; YK 168
84:6	YK 555
84:8	YK 661
84:13	YK 412
85:10–11	RH 273; YK 287
86:8	RH 227; YK 255
86:11	YK 356
88:19	YK 215
89:3	YK 359
89:16	YK 671
90	YK 579
90:3	YK 555
90:6	YK 555
92	YK 585
92:2	YK 396
92:3	YK 39
92:13	YK 166
93	YK 166
93:1	RH 203
95:6	RH 110; YK 138
97:11	YK 16, 224
98:6	RH 2, 204, 280
98:9	RH 280
99:4	RH 204
99:5	RH 229
99:9	RH 229
100:2	YK 501
100:2–4	YK 642
102:1	YK 324
102:2–3	YK 549
102:15	RH 61
103:11	YK 412
103:13	YK 412
103:14	RH 181; YK 428

103:15–18	YK 546
104	YK 2
104:1–2	RH 106; YK 132
104:24	YK 494
104:27	YK 379
104:35	YK 151
106:45	RH 265
111:5	RH 265
111:10	YK 223
112:9	YK 57
115:16	RH 139
115:18	RH 133–34, 303, 305–6; YK 169
116:12	YK 586
117	YK 22
118:5	RH 35; YK 555
118:14	YK 325
118:17	YK 585
118:19	YK 613, 629, 670
118:20	YK 641
118:29	RH 235
119:89	YK 642
119:105	YK 125
119:160	RH 161
119:165	YK 142
120:1	YK 468
121	RH 8, 92, 131; YK 140, 556
121:1	YK 603
121:1–2	RH 131; YK 457
121:5	RH 177
122	YK 451
126	RH 61
126:2	YK 478
126:5	YK 123, 501, 585, 607
128:2	YK 665
128:3	YK 497
130	YK 67
130:1–2	YK 551
130:6	RH 165; YK 460
130:7	YK 473
130:8	YK 470
131:1–2	YK 486
131:2	YK 579
131:3	YK 489
132:4–5	YK 504

Index of Rabbinic Citations

RH = Rosh HaShanah volume; YK = Yom Kippur volume

Index of Text Authors and Authorities Cited

RH = Rosh HaShanah volume; YK = Yom Kippur volume

Table of Poems for Rosh HaShanah

By First Words

Table of Poems for Yom Kippur

Table of Poems and Songs, by Service

See also Index of Biblical Citations, s.v. Psalms

Table of Readings Related to Key Liturgical Rubrics

NOTES

NOTES

NOTES

NOTES

NOTES

NOTES

NOTES

CCAR Press

CENTRAL CONFERENCE OF AMERICAN RABBIS • SINCE 1889

מחזור לימים הנוראי

משכן הנפש

MISHKAN HANEFESH
Machzor for the Days of Awe

Edited by Rabbi Edwin Goldberg,
Rabbi Janet Marder, Rabbi Sheldon
Marder, and Rabbi Leon Morris,
with Rabbi Elaine Zecher, Cantor Evan
Kent, and Rabbi Peter Berg

*Two Volume Set: Rosh HaShanah and Yom Kippur
Standard Size, Hardcover*

Mishkan HaNefesh: Machzor for the Days of Awe offers meaningful liturgy for both regular service attendees and those new to Jewish spirituality and practice. Providing an accessible guide through the journey of *t'shuvah* (repentance) and *cheshbon hanefesh* (self-reflection), it bridges the personal and the communal, as well as the ritual and the ethical dimensions of *Yamim HaNoraim*.

SPECIAL FEATURES

- Fully transliterated liturgy
- Expanded options for Torah readings
- Study texts that provide background and context
- Contemporary poetry and alternative readings
- Rich commentary drawing from Jewish tradition
- A range of theological possibilities
- New translations that capture the beauty of the Hebrew
- Original woodblock art by acclaimed artist Joel Shapiro
- Includes essays by the leading Reform Movement thinkers

For more information and to order, go to ccarpress.org or call 212-972-3636 x241.
| CCAR | 355 Lexington Avenue | New York, NY 10017 | ravblog.ccarnet.org

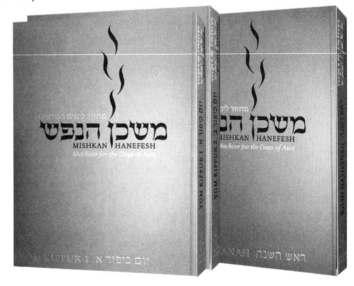

מחזור לימים הנוראים

משכן הנפש

MISHKAN HANEFESH
Machzor for the Days of Awe

Pulpit Edition

Edited by Rabbi Edwin Goldberg, Rabbi Janet Marder, Rabbi Sheldon Marder, and Rabbi Leon Morris, with Rabbi Elaine Zecher, Cantor Evan Kent, and Rabbi Peter Berg

This oversized pulpit edition is meant to be used by service leaders. The pagination matches that of the two volume set.

CCAR Press

CENTRAL CONFERENCE OF AMERICAN RABBIS • SINCE 1889

Shirei Mishkan HaNefesh

Project Editor: Cantor Steven Weiss

Editor: Joel Eglash

Chair of Editorial Committee:
Cantor Susan Caro

The compendium of new musical compositions, *Shirei Mishkan HaNefesh*, developed by the American Conference of Cantors in partnership with the CCAR Press, reflects the same core values as *Mishkan HaNefesh*. Like the new *machzor*, this collection of original musical compositions gives voice to new liturgy and expands upon the familiar themes that have remained with us from generation to generation. A great High Holy Day resource!

Includes two copies of the volume for the service leader and the accompanist.

שירי משכן הנפש

SHIREI MISHKAN HANEFESH

An Anthology of Music for the High Holy Days

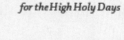

CCAR Press

CENTRAL CONFERENCE OF AMERICAN RABBIS • SINCE 1889

MACHZOR: CHALLENGE AND CHANGE, VOLUME I

Edited by Rabbi Hara E. Person
and Rabbi Sara Newman Rich

After having developed and published a new High Holy Day *machzor*, the CCAR invites Reform Jews to engage in study on related themes. This collection includes a wealth of material for individual or group study, including presentations on *Un'taneh Tokef*, *Kol Nidrei*, and *Avinu Malkeinu*, High Holy Day-themed essays from back issues of the CCAR Journal, and discussion questions.

TOPICS INCLUDE:

- *Avinu Malkeinu*
- *Un'taneh Tokef*
- *Kol Nidrei*
- Related Essays from *CCAR Journal: The Reform Jewish Quarterly*, Spring 2009

MACHZOR:

Challenge and Change
Resource Pack
for Congregational Study

CENTRAL CONFERENCE
OF AMERICAN RABBIS

CCAR Press

CENTRAL CONFERENCE OF AMERICAN RABBIS • SINCE 1889

Machzor: Challenge and Change, Volume 2

Edited by Rabbis Hara E. Person and Adena Kemper,
with Rabbi Liz Piper-Goldberg

The CCAR has just recently developed and published the new Reform machzor, the biggest liturgical project of this generation. *Machzor: Challenge and Change*, V2 is a comprehensive resource that provides material for communal engagement and study of the *machzor*. The book includes presentations from scholars and thought leaders on liturgical themes and concepts such as *N'ilah, Avodah, Eilah Ezkarah*, and High Holy Day Torah portions, as well as *machzor*-related essays from the CCAR Journal. It also includes discussion questions throughout. A terrific adult-study packet.

TOPICS INCLUDE:

- Traditional Torah Readings: *Akeidah* and *Nitzavim*

- Traditional Torah Readings Reconsidered

- Shofar Service

- *Seder HaAvodah*

- *Eileh Ezkarah*

- *Yizkor*

- *N'ilah*

- *Hin'ni*

- Between Faith and Protest: Presentations from the CCAR Convention 2013 Long Beach

- Related Articles and Poems from the CCAR Journal

MACHZOR
Challenge and Change,
Volume 2

Preparing for the New Machzor
and for the High Holy Days

CENTRAL CONFERENCE OF AMERICAN RABBIS

For more information and to order, go to ccarpress.org or call 212-972-3636 x241.
| CCAR | 355 Lexington Avenue | New York, NY 10017 | ravblog.ccarnet.org